Armed
and
Dangerous

DELIVERANCE AND SPIRITUAL WARFARE MANUAL

Armed
and
Dangerous

HENRY B. SHAFFER, SR.

Cover design by Rebeccacovers of FIVERR
Interior design by Aalishaa of FIVERR
Editing by Pamela Scholtes

Published by The Fiery Sword Publications, Lexington, SC, United States of America

Hardcover ISBN 9798876263865
softcover ISBN 9798876263667 (color)
softcover ISBN 9798876264732 (blk/wht)

Books › Religion & Spirituality › Occult & Paranormal › Supernatural
Books › Religion & Spirituality › Religious Studies › Counseling
Books › Religion & Spirituality › Worship & Devotion › Inspirational

TABLE OF CONTENTS

Section I

TABLE OF CONTENTS

Section II

Section III

PREFACE

"Thou art my battle axe and weapons of war: for with thee will I break in pieces the nations, and with thee will I destroy kingdoms (Jeremiah 51:20, KJV)."

There are many books written on deliverance from demonic spirits. The books range from just a few pages to hundreds of pages. Once a person digests all the deliverance information, many are left questioning how one performs deliverance on a person. After many years in deliverance ministry, I found myself teaching the concepts of this freedom ministry. Following the outlines of others, I still did not find an effective procedure to follow. The goal is to produce an outline to remove the strongman of a demonic kingdom within a person's mind, will, emotions, and body. With God's direction, I developed an effective, to-the-point deliverance procedure manual. This is a step-by-step instruction manual on how to conduct an effective deliverance.

ACKNOWLEDGMENTS

I want to acknowledge the many people who influenced the ministry and have worked tirelessly to set people free from demonic strongholds.

My childhood pastor, The Reverend Eddie Renew—I saw him cast out demons as a child. My parents, Henry and Helen Shaffer, who loved us so much they wanted us to have a saving relationship with Jesus Christ, Lord and Savior. God sent Dr. James and Marty Fent, who came along at the right time when deliverance started at University Parkway Church in Aiken, South Carolina.

Evangelist Bea Medlin, a general of the faith in deliverance and miracles, who mentored me and shared many secrets of spiritual warfare, casting out demons, and believing God for miracles; and for receiving the mantle of deliverance from Sister Medlin.

The staff and church family of University Parkway, Spiritual Freedom Network ministers, board members of Spiritual Freedom Network, and volunteers who endured hours of sermons on deliverance and set thousands free.

Special acknowledgment to Associate Pastor of University Parkway, Reverend Bill and (spouse) Phyllis George, Treasurer Dana and (spouse) Bill Turner, Personal Assistant and Church Secretary Rachel and (spouse) Walter Glanton, who work behind the scenes to coordinate this deliverance ministry.

My family, Brother Rev. T.D. (spouse Rose) Shaffer, Sister Kay (spouse Walter) Brend, Brother Guy Shaffer, Brother Michael (spouse Kathy) Johnson, Brother Lee Shaffer; my children, Henry Bo Shaffer Jr. (spouse Candy) Shaffer, Christine (spouse Alex) Locay, and daughter Amy Shaffer, and family members who supported with monies and prayers over the years of ministry.

Special acknowledgment to my spouse and best friend, Fran Wylds Shaffer. In our 48-year marriage, you loved me when I wasn't loveable, and always supported my life and ministry. You are a woman of God and a demon terrorist, as well.

DEDICATION

To my youngest daughter, Amy Lynn Shaffer, who died at age 40. Her Mom, Fran, and I, did our best to help her recover from drugs and a life of demonic assignments against her. We didn't know how to fight using deliverance, at that time.

God says that revenge belongs to him.

> "Dearly beloved, avenge not yourselves, but rather give place unto wrath: for it is written, Vengeance is mine; I will repay, saith the Lord (Romans 12:19, KJV)."

God told me to build Him an army. That's my job. I will complete my assignment. I have this promise from God's Word how He will use us if we let him:

> "Thou art my battle axe and weapons of war: for with thee will I break in pieces the nations, and with thee will I destroy kingdoms; (Demonic Kingdoms) (Jeremiah 51:20)."

Every time during a deliverance session, I tell the demon to carry a message to the pit, "When you get there, tell hell the power has returned to the church." Hey, battle axes, are you ready to fight and make the devil pay? I am not a pushover!

FOREWORD

As we navigate through life, we are faced with various challenges that sometimes leave us feeling helpless and powerless. In such moments, we often seek divine intervention and turn to the power of prayer. However, some situations require more than just prayers. They need a deeper understanding of the spiritual realm and the necessary tools. *"Armed and Dangerous: Deliverance and Spiritual Warfare Manual"* by Pastor Henry Shaffer seeks to provide Christians with a better understanding of spiritual warfare and how to effectively engage.

This book is a must-read for anyone desiring to live a victorious Christian life, free from the oppression of demonic forces. Pastor Henry Shaffer, a seasoned minister with years of experience in deliverance ministry, shares practical insights and teachings on supernatural healing and casting out demons from Christian believers and the demonically oppressed. He draws from his wealth of knowledge and experience to give readers powerful and effective tools for engaging in spiritual warfare.

"Armed and Dangerous" provides a comprehensive understanding of the biblical basis for deliverance ministry, dispelling common misconceptions and misunderstandings about the topic. It also explores the different types of demonic attacks, including physical, emotional, and mental oppression, and how to identify and over-

come them. Pastor Henry Shaffer's engaging writing style makes it easy for readers to follow along and understand the concepts and principles he presents.

I highly recommend this book to anyone seeking to deepen their spiritual understanding and effectively engage in spiritual warfare. This is a valuable resource for pastors, ministry leaders, and Christian believers. It equips them with the knowledge and tools necessary to overcome the powers of darkness and live a victorious Christian life. I am confident readers will find this book informative, inspiring, and transformational.

I have personally had the privilege of working alongside Pastor Shaffer and putting into practice the principles and teachings presented. As a result, I have witnessed firsthand the manifestation of signs and wonders as demons were cast out and the sick were healed. I have seen people once bound by cancer, tumors, migraines, and cold sores receive miraculous healing through God's power. I have even seen bones pop back into place. Individuals are set free from the spirit of Beelzebub, Lilith, anger, stubbornness, witchcraft, marine spirit, spirit spouse, generational curses, word curses, and Polynesian gods.

The efficacy of deliverance ministry is broader than just adults. We have also seen children as young as two years old delivered from demonic influence. It is truly remarkable to see the transformation in lives once freed from oppression's chains. The stories of people set free from demonic influence are truly inspiring and serve as a testament to God's power.

The structure and detailed information shared in *"Armed and Dangerous"*, and our own experiences demonstrate that deliverance ministry is not just reserved for a select few. It is available to all who believe in the power of Jesus Christ of Nazareth. As Pastor Shaffer explains, the key to effective deliverance ministry lies in understanding the biblical principles of spiritual warfare and engaging in it with the authority and power given to us through Jesus Christ.

"Armed and Dangerous: Deliverance with Pastor Henry Shaffer" is a timely and much-needed resource for Christians seeking to engage in spiritual warfare and overcome the powers of darkness. It is a solution to the end-time prophecy of Christians falling away from the faith. I am confident readers will find this book informative, practical, and life-changing.

In these end-times, the Bible warns us of the great falling away of believers from the faith. It is becoming increasingly important for Christians to deeply understand spiritual warfare and the tools necessary to navigate the spiritual realm. This book is the answer to this prophetic warning, providing readers with a biblical understanding of deliverance ministry and the importance of engaging in spiritual warfare.

"Armed" serves as a guide to help Christians identify and overcome the spirit of deception that has crept into the Church. It provides practical tools and strategies for testing the spirits and saturating the spirit-man with God's Word. By doing so, believers can equip themselves to withstand the devil's schemes and live a victorious Christian life.

This is more than just a book—it is a call to action. It challenges us to take the work of spiritual warfare seriously and to actively engage in it. It reminds us that our battle is not against flesh and blood but against the powers of darkness seeking to destroy us. As we read this book, let us be inspired and empowered to take up our armor and engage in the work of delivering individuals from demonic oppression.

Sai Tagovailoa-Amosa, Senior Pastor
Message Of Peace Ministry Outreach, Ewa Beach, HI

INTRODUCTION

Most importantly, you should choose this deliverance manual as an outline for deliverance sessions. It is a practical approach to removing the strongman as described in this book. Inside, you will find a strategy that supports the biblical battle plan to remove demonic spirits. This strategy was developed after hours of intense deliverance sessions. Holy Spirit directed this strategy to diminish hours of deliverance into a concise step-by-step plan with detailed instructions on how to ensure demonic spirits have evacuated their home [the person]. This book contains a working deliverance procedure, a how-to book for taking a person through deliverance. After being trained by the contents of this book, many deliverance ministers report that this procedure is superior to others they have been trained on. Step by step, this book is laid out, ensuring that forgiveness and repentance will open the door to remove Satan's key demons and strongholds trying to thwart a successful deliverance. By moving from forgiveness to mind control, you will be able to remove the most prideful demon called the king of all the children of pride, Leviathan. Many deliverance teams gasp as they try to remove this powerful foe. Follow the provided material, and you can be confident the deliverance session will usher the candidate freedom once complete. Always be open to Holy Spirit guidance to lead you in deliverance endeavors. That is how this outline was developed.

DISCLAIMER

"Caution, Warning, and Danger" denote a more progressive state of endangerment. A serious word of caution before attempting deliverance using the "Armed and Dangerous' deliverance procedure on your own. In the Scriptures, there was an attempt to deliver a person. The group's name is the "Sons of Sceva" referenced in Acts 19:11-18.

[11] And God wrought special miracles by the hands of Paul: [12] So that from his body were brought unto the sick handkerchiefs or aprons, and the diseases departed from them, and the evil spirits went out of them. [13] Then certain of the vagabond Jews, exorcists, took upon them to call over them which had evil spirits the name of the Lord Jesus, saying, We adjure you by Jesus whom Paul preacheth. [14] And there were seven sons of one Sceva, a Jew, and chief of the priests, which did so. [15] And the evil spirit answered and said, Jesus I know, and Paul I know; but who are ye? [16] And the man in whom the evil spirit was leaped on them, and overcame them, and prevailed against them, so that they fled out of that house naked and wounded. [17] And this was known to all the Jews and Greeks also dwelling at Ephesus; and fear fell on them all, and the

name of the Lord Jesus was magnified. [18] And many that believed came, and confessed, and shewed their deeds.

This story shows how the demons did not know this Sceva. Historians reveal that Sceva was a High Priest, exorcists, who had seven sons who carried out an exorcism on a demonized man. The demons did not know them, or the author of their presumed authority. The name Sceva denotes one who is willing and prepared, but in this case, they were not prepared. They were not ready and did not know it.

Are you ready to proceed? If yes, spiritually consider your relationship with Jesus and the condition of your faith level. You must be more than willing; you must be qualified. Jesus made sure his disciples knew how to cast out demons.

Recommendations To Consider Before Proceeding

1. **WARNING: THIS IS NOT CHILD'S PLAY OR ENTERTAINMENT.**

2. You are embarking into the supernatural ministry of casting out spiritual malevolent demons.

3. You will be disrupting to kingdom of darkness that has built its' stronghold around a person, family, church, business, etc.

4. The spiritual condition of a person attempting to minister deliverance should be evaluated before using this armed and dangerous deliverance procedure.

5. You MUST be a Christian on believing grounds, living as a Christian with an active prayer life, walking in the light of the Scriptures.

6. Engaging the enemy with less than being baptized in the Holy Ghost with the evidence of speaking in tongues puts us at the place where Jesus told His disciples to go to the upper room and wait for the empowering of the Holy Ghost. How important is this? You shall receive power.

   Acts 1:4-8: And, being assembled together with them, commanded them that they should not depart from Jerusalem, but wait for the promise of the Father, which, saith he, ye have heard of me.

   Acts 1:5: For John truly baptized with water; but ye shall be baptized with the Holy Ghost not many days hence.

   Acts 1:6: When they therefore were come together, they asked of him, saying, Lord, wilt thou at this time restore again the kingdom to Israel?

   Acts 1:7: And he said unto them, It is not for you to know the times or the seasons, which the Father hath put in his own power.

   Acts 1:8: But ye shall receive power, after that the Holy Ghost is come upon you: and ye shall be witnesses unto me both in Jerusalem, and in all Judaea, and in Samaria, and unto the uttermost part of the earth.

7. Demons can transfer from person to person—to and from the person attempting to be set free and from the deliverance minster. There is a way to prevent this unwanted transfer—it's in this manual. Forbid the transference of any spirit in any way whatsoever.

8. Demons will re-enforce their strongholds in the person you are trying to set free. Warn them they must guard their spiritual man.

9. Expect spiritual attacks on yourself, family, friends, pets, and belongings for trying to set people free.

10. Relationship struggles may develop.

11. Demons will come back with a vengeance. The return of an unclean spirit will soon happen after deliverance. You must be on guard and not let this spirit reenter.

   Matthew 12:43-45: When the unclean spirit is gone out of a man, he walketh through dry places, seeking rest, and findeth none.

   Matthew 12:44: Then he saith, I will return into my house from whence I came out; and when he is come, he findeth it empty, swept, and garnished.

   Matthew 12:45: Then goeth he, and taketh with himself seven other spirits more wicked than himself, and they enter in and dwell there: and the last state of that man is worse than the first. Even so shall it be also unto this wicked generation   .

12. You must be on guard. By choosing to proceed you are accepting the **danger** presented in scripture.

   1 Peter 5:8: Be sober, be vigilant; because your adversary the devil, as a roaring lion, walketh about, seeking whom he may devour.

SECTION I

Basics

CHAPTER ONE

HOW TO ENGAGE THE ENEMY

Deliverance Strategy and Battle Plan

1. **A Call for Help**

    Good morning, Pastor Henry. My mom led me to your ministry. My family really needs help. My husband and I adopted two kids about four years ago. They have gotten so difficult that I am in tears starting my day. They don't respond to any form of discipline and only get angry. My daughter screams and growls. Her eyes turn black or squint with defiance. I'm growing weary in the spiritual and physical battle. It's been especially bad for a month now. My home phone is_____. I'm in _____. Please help. God bless.

2. **Strategy**: the art of planning and directing overall military operations and movements in a war or battle.

    "Blessed be the LORD my strength which teacheth my hands to war, and my fingers to fight (Psalm 144:1)."

3. The Word of God

"Is not my word like as a fire? saith the LORD; and like a hammer that breaketh the rock in pieces (Jeremiah 23:29)."

4. Prayer

"But ye, beloved, building up yourselves on your most holy faith, praying in the Holy Ghost (Jude 1:20)."

5. Fasting

"Howbeit this kind goeth not out but by prayer and fasting (Matthew 17:21)."

6. Humility

"Likewise, ye younger, submit yourselves unto the elder. Yea, all of you be subject one to another, and be clothed with humility: for God resisteth the proud, and giveth grace to the humble (I Peter 5:5)."

7. Authority

"And they were all amazed, insomuch that they questioned among themselves, saying, What thing is this? what new doctrine is this? for with authority commandeth he even the unclean spirits, and they do obey him (Mark 1:27)."

8. Binding and Loosing

"Verily I say unto you, whatsoever ye shall bind on earth shall be bound in heaven: and whatsoever ye shall loose on earth shall be loosed in heaven (Matthew 18:18)."

9. **The Plan Revealed—Steps to Cast out the Strongman**

    a. There are five significant steps to remove one of the fiercest demons, called Leviathan.

    b. Removal of unforgiveness, bitterness, stubbornness, mind control, and leviathan's shield are critical to setting a person free from the control and torment of leviathan.

10. As you begin this deliverance session, reference appendix four.

Soul Ties

1. Emphasis must be placed on breaking soul ties.

2. Good soul ties[1] are formed when two or more persons become bonded together.

3. Some soul ties are good, and others are evil; some are holy, and some are ungodly.

4. Good soul ties are found between husband and wife, parents and children, brothers and sisters, friends with friends, Christians and the Body of Christ.

5. Ties in marriage are found in Ephesians 5:22-32.

6. Demonic soul ties are perversions of good soul ties. Satan cannot go beyond the legal right given to him by sin and perversion of soul ties.

7. Soul ties are invisible bands [yokes] in the spiritual realm. They can be sexual, emotional, physical, or spiritual.

---

1 Soul Ties, Breaking Chains of Darkness page 133, Dr. James Fent

8. Ungodly sexual soul ties are formed when two people have sex outside biblical marriage.

9. Emotional soul ties are developed through co-dependency with another person.

10. Physical soul ties are formed through a slave mentality.

11. Spiritual soul ties are formed by mentors, spiritual leaders, and deceptive practices.

12. Evil companions, perverted soul ties, and soul ties with the dead must be broken.

13. Prayer to break Soul Ties:

I accept God's forgiveness for each sin I participated. Father, I break all soul ties formed through inordinate affection for animals, family members where there is control and possessiveness, and corrupt and depraved companions who have influenced me in perverse ways. I break soul ties with the dead and from prolonged mourning over deceased loved ones. I break church related soul ties where I have been a part of church cliques, idolized a pastor or church leader above Christ, or been controlled by anyone in leadership in Jesus' name.

NOTES

NOTES

NOTES

CHAPTER TWO

UNFORGIVENESS

Begin by removing the unforgiveness [unwillingness to forgive]. Humility, repentance, and forgiveness ensure God will fulfill His promise of deliverance.

1. This is where forgiveness is exposed and demons of unforgiveness are revealed. You must forgive all people. In Mark 11:25-26, Jesus reveals an essential principle how important it is to forgive.

   "And when ye stand praying, forgive, if ye have ought against any: that your Father also which is in heaven may forgive you your trespasses. But if ye do not forgive, neither will your Father which is in heaven forgive your trespasses (Mark 11:25-26)."

2. If we desire forgiveness from God for our sins, we must forgive others first.

3. In Matthew 18:23-35, the judgment of the unforgiving servant was to be turned over to the tormenter's torture.

[23] Therefore is the kingdom of heaven likened unto a certain king, which would take account of his servants. [24] And when he had begun to reckon, one was brought unto him, which owed him ten thousand talents. [25] But forasmuch as he had not to pay, his lord commanded him to be sold, and his wife, and children, and all that he had, and payment to be made. [26] The servant therefore fell down, and worshipped him, saying, Lord, have patience with me, and I will pay thee all. [27] Then the lord of that servant was moved with compassion, and loosed him, and forgave him the debt. [28] But the same servant went out, and found one of his fellow servants, which owed him an hundred pence: and he laid hands on him, and took him by the throat, saying, Pay me that thou owest. [29] And his fellow servant fell down at his feet, and besought him, saying, Have patience with me, and I will pay thee all. [30] And he would not: but went and cast him into prison, till he should pay the debt. [31] So when his fellow servants saw what was done, they were very sorry, and came and told unto their lord all that was done. [32] Then his lord, after that he had called him, said unto him, O thou wicked servant, I forgave thee all that debt, because thou desiredst me: [33] Shouldest not thou also have had compassion on thy fellow servant, even as I had pity on thee? [34] And his lord was wroth, and delivered him to the tormentors, till he should pay all that was due unto him. [35] So likewise shall my heavenly Father do also unto you, if ye from your hearts forgive not everyone his brother their trespasses (Matthew 18:23-35).

4. This is equivalent to being turned over to the torment of demons on a child of God for not forgiving trespasses against them.

5. Forgiving a person is not an emotion; it is an act of the will. Here is how to verbalize:

   "I forgive _____ for what they caused. As an act of my will, I now release them of all guilt, bitterness, and resentment. I cancel their debt owed to me. I love them; I forgive as You have forgiven me. In the name of Jesus, Amen."

6. Identify problem areas that harbor unforgiveness:

   a. Family hurts, disputes, divorce, legal matters, etc.
   b. Employment quarrels, fights, disappointment.
   c. Church hurt and disappointments.
   d. School rejection causing unforgiveness—first grade all the way to graduation of second tier schooling.

7. This is where you will find more spirits of unforgiveness hiding. You will see the person reliving the hurt associated with these events that opened them to harbor unforgiveness.

8. An emotional release is this step's purpose. Forgiving others and themselves from guilt and shame associated with their life is required to remove tormentors.

9. Unforgiveness opens doors to the tormentors. The tormentors left behind continue to hide and will bring unwanted oppression.

10. Look for NDA [Non-Disclosed Agreements] in lawsuits requiring a person not to mention names or places of hurt.

NOTES

NOTES

NOTES

CHAPTER THREE

BITTERNESS

This spirit brings poison which deposits into the bones and joints that causes arthritis.

1. Bitterness[2] is one spirit that enters through hard bondage.

   "And they made their lives bitter with hard bondage, in morter, and in brick, and in all manner of service in the field: all their service, wherein they made them serve, was with rigour (Exodus 1:14)."

2. Unforgiveness leads to bitterness. This is the 2x2 spiritual principles to reinforce a stronghold.

3. There is a relationship between bitterness and sickness. A root of bitterness can result in poison that bears gall and wormwood.

   "Lest there should be among you man, or woman, or family, or tribe, whose heart turneth away this day from the LORD our God, to go and serve the gods of these nations; lest there

2 Page 213 – 215 John Eckhardt Spiritual Warfare and Deliverance Manual.

should be among you a root that beareth gall and wormwood (Deuteronomy 29:18)."

4. Bitterness is linked with envy and strife according to James 3:14, which states, "But if ye have bitter envying and strife in your hearts, glory not, and lie not against the truth (James 3:14)."

5. Bitterness can enter parents through foolish children.

   "A foolish son is a grief to his father, and bitterness to her that bare him. A person can be in the "gall of bitterness" makes its path to witchcraft and sorcery (Proverbs 17:25)."

6. Bitterness can bring:

   a. Arthritis
   b. Body pain
   c. Cancer
   d. Division
   e. Joint pain
   f. Strife
   g. Swelling in joints

7. A person can speak word curses by complaining and bring dryness to the bones.

8. A broken spirit can dry out the bones according to Proverbs 17:22, which reads, "A merry heart doeth good like a medicine: but a broken spirit drieth the bones."

9. Harboring unforgiveness grants bitterness a legal right to enter a person.

10. A broken spirit is the result of sorrow and grief.

"A merry heart maketh a cheerful countenance: but by sorrow of the heart the spirit is broken (Proverbs 15:13)."

11. The broken spirit affects the marrow, and opens the door for spirits of arthritis, bone cancer, and serious blood diseases such as leukemia. Evil spirits can vex the bones (Luke 6:18, Psalm 6:2).

12. Envy and jealousy can cause the bones to rot.

"A sound heart is the life of the flesh: but envy the rottenness of the bones (Proverbs 14:30)."

13. Witchcraft curses can affect the bones.

"As he loved cursing, so let it come unto him: as he delighted not in blessing, so let it be far from him. [18] As he clothed himself with cursing like as with his garment, so let it come into his bowels like water, and like oil into his bones (Psalm 109:17-18)."

14. Spirits of pain operating in the bones can be the result of pride.

"That he may withdraw man from his purpose and hide pride from man. [18] He keepeth back his soul from the pit, and his life from perishing by the sword. [19] He is chastened also with pain upon his bed, and the multitude of his bones with strong pain (Job 33:17-19)."

15. Drought of summer, dry bones, no moisture in the bones, etc. all cause unhealthy bones. Deliverance from unforgiveness, hurt, sorrow, and grief will cause the bones to rejoice.

"And my soul shall be joyful in the LORD: it shall rejoice in his salvation. [10] All my bones shall say, LORD, who is like unto thee, which deliverest the poor from him that is too strong for him, yea, the poor and the needy from him that spoileth him (Psalm 35:9-10)."

16. When ministering to individuals with bone problems, be sure to have them renounce bitterness and unforgiveness, and come against spirits of grief, sadness, broken heart, rottenness, envy, jealousy, bitterness, root of bitterness, unforgiveness, hatred, arthritis, rheumatism, pain, pride, curses, mind control linked with memory recall [a spirit that constantly reminds the person of hurt], and infirmities in the marrow, joints, and muscles.[3]

17. Anoint the feet, moving the Bible along to the ankles, knees, thighs, hips, back, fingers, wrists, elbows, neck, shoulders, to the throat.

18. Call out arthritis and joint pain. Bitterness and arthritis work together. It's the 2x2 spiritual principle.

19. Have the individual come out of agreement with hurt, deep hurt, resentment, and anger.

20. Many will spit and report a very bitter taste in their mouth.

21. Getting to the root of bitterness is most important.

---

3 John Eckhardt page 196 Appendix A

NOTES

NOTES

NOTES

CHAPTER FOUR

~

STUBBORNNESS

The removal of Stubbornness is the key to unlock the chains of bondage. Stubbornness—Destroying Stubborn Demons and Strongholds[4]

1. Stubbornness is a stronghold you may think will never be broken. God will deliver you from every trick and wile of the devil.

2. Definition of Stubborn:
   a. unreasonably or perversely unyielding: mulish
   b. justifiably unyielding: resolute
   c. suggestive or typical of a strong stubborn nature a stubborn jaw
   d. performed or carried on in an unyielding, obstinate, or persistent manner stubborn effort
   e. difficult to handle, manage, or treat a stubborn cold
   f. lasting stubborn facts

---

4 Reference Page 118 - 123 John Eckhardt – Deliverance and Spiritual Warfare Manual. (DSWM)

3. Satan has a plot to keep you in bondage, but God has a plan to deliver you. Stubbornness is a strong spirit in the arsenal of Satan's kingdom.

    "And Moses said unto the people, Fear ye not, stand still, and see the salvation of the LORD, which he will shew to you to-day: for the Egyptians whom ye have seen today, ye shall see them again no more forever (Exodus 14:13)."

4. There are different kinds of demons; some are weak, strong, dense, intelligent, and stubborn.

5. Some demons always put up a fight and it takes a lot more strength and anointing to remove the demon or demonic stronghold.

6. *"This kind of demon"*—some spirits will require a person to fast to break a stubborn spirit.

    [18] And Jesus rebuked the devil; and he departed out of him: and the child was cured from that very hour. [19] Then came the disciples to Jesus apart, and said, Why could not we cast him out? [20] And Jesus said unto them, Because of your unbelief: for verily I say unto you, If ye have faith as a grain of mustard seed, ye shall say unto this mountain, Remove hence to yonder place; and it shall remove; and nothing shall be impossible unto you. [21] Howbeit this kind goeth not out but by prayer and fasting (Matthew 17:18-21).

7. This means there are different kinds of demons. Some are stronger not as easy to remove because they are defiant and deep rooted.

8. Stubbornness can be the result of a generational curse loosed on a family's bloodline.

9. Word curses spoken by parents, friends, co-workers, etc. can open this door to oppress an individual.

10. The deeper the root in the soil, the harder to pull out the rooted plant.

11. It is notably easier to remove stubbornness from a baby, child, or teenager. Once a person has developed attitude or personality of stubbornness and it continues throughout their life, it can be difficult to set a person free from this mindset.

12. Obstinate: refusing to change one's mind or course of action despite pressure to do so; unyielding or resolute.

13. Synonyms for obstinate, characterized by a refusal to change one's mind or course of action:

    a. Dogged
    b. Earnestness
    c. Persistent
    d. Prejudice

14. Satan will use this stubbornness to stop a deliverance session.

    a. Bring to naught
    b. Hard
    c. Hinder
    d. Mule
    e. Resist
    f. Stall
    g. Stop

15. During the deliverance session, if there is no sign of deliverance or movement of this spirit, use the following:

    a. Address stubbornness and call it out.
    b. This is a key removal because it could hold up the deliverance.
    c. Removal of this spirit is crucial.
    d. Stubbornness can be used by a strongman to hold up the participant's deliverance.
    e. Cast out this spirit in the opening moves of deliverance.

16. Call out hardheaded, bull spirit, I must have it my way, mule spirit, unyielding are classed with stubbornness.

17. Use anointing oil if necessary to break the yoke of stubbornness.

"And it shall come to pass in that day, that his burden shall be taken away from off thy shoulder, and his yoke from off thy neck, and the yoke shall be destroyed because of the anointing (Isaiah 10:17)."

18. List of stubborn spirits: religious, lust, addiction, bitterness, anger, poverty, and Goliath.

19. Life Lesson: I've seen a person start laughing when stubbornness comes up. It said, "I don't come out that easily. No, I'm not coming out. I've been here a long time." I asked, "Do you have a legal right?" It responded, "No." I said, "You are an invader, a trespasser, then you have to go." Out it went.

20. Similar spirits to call out:

    a. Bull
    b. Feisty
    c. Hard Rock
    d. Hardheaded
    e. I must have it my way.
    f. My way is the best way
    g. Strong willed

NOTES

NOTES

NOTES

CHAPTER FIVE

MIND CONTROL

The removal of mind control is a major component in a person's deliverance.

1. Mind control[5] spirits can control the mind and affect the way a person conducts life affairs.

2. If evil spirits can control the thoughts, they can defeat the individual.

    "For as he thinketh in his heart, so is he: eat and drink, saith he to thee; but his heart is not with thee (Proverbs 23:7)."

3. People can receive mind control spirits through music [rock, jazz, disco, etc.], meditation, reading certain books, drugs and alcohol—anything that alters the mind and breaks the hedge of a healthy mind.

    "He that diggeth a pit shall fall into it; and whoso breaketh an hedge, a serpent shall bite him (Ecclesiastes 10:8)."

---

5 Reference Page 230 John Eckhardt – (DSWM)

© DeliveranceWithPastorHenry

4. Passivity, control by another person, mind exposure to false teachings, psychology, pornography, and so on.

5. Mind control spirits can be inherited.

6. They have tentacles and resemble creatures such as an octopus or squid.

7. Migraine headaches can be caused by mind-control spirits.

8. Mind control works with insanity, mental illness, schizophrenia, intellectualism, and a host of others that operate in the mind.

9. Mind control also gives a person the ability to control the mind of another.

10. Many pastors and church leaders have very powerful mind-control spirits. False teachers and cults also use mind control to keep people bound to them.

11. These spirits hate anointing the forehead with oil, and this is helpful in binding them.

12. Also, anointing the top, back, and sides or temples, is sometimes necessary.

13. When a person receives deliverance from mind control, the person is able to think clearly, some for the first time in their lives.

14. In attacking mind control, come against the tentacles by asking the Lord to send angels to sever them.

15. Spirits can be represented by sea creatures[6], land animals, insects, and flying species.

16. Testimony received on 10-7-2022 related to mind control:

---

6 Reference page 180 John Eckhardt (DSWM)

Dear Pastor Henry,

I am from South Africa, what I can say is that Almighty God is moving in your ministry.

I would like to book for online deliverance please kindly for deliverance from the leviathan spirit and just for total deliverance. My situation is dire, been trying to get fully delivered for years. At this point I need real help and I know I've found it in your ministry.

I love Jesus and I always try to do right in my walk with him. I've been doing warfare prayers to break free from this and I embrace my relationship with Holy Spirit. I do see changes recently because I spend more time in the presence of God and fasting and reading of His Word. I believe that when I went through your session on YouTube I got deliverance from the octopus, mind control spirit. I was sneezing non-stop, burping, and spiting a lot. My story is so long, and it points to this spirit for sure. I tried to get deliverance through going to places of deliverance, but it's not done with a heart like you do. I would manifest but that would be cut short. When you explain the octopus, it verifies that's happening in my head and in my life. God has called me to my nations but the enemy if fighting me really bad. I have made up my mind that next year I will visit South Carolina with my family because we need so much help. Thank you for listening. I look forward to your response in Jesus Christ's name.

Kind regards,

South Africa

NOTES

NOTES

NOTES

CHAPTER SIX

PRECURSOR TO CHAPTER SEVEN

Using Natural Enemies To Defeat The Enemies Of God In Spiritual Warfare

A. LESSON: Defeating the enemy with the enemies of the enemy.

God uses natural enemies to defeat a demonic spirit that was using Pharaoh to keep God's people in bondage.

God used natural pestilence to defeat Pharaoh during the children of Israel's exodus. Moses was called to release ten plagues, which attacked the lives of those in Egypt and the Land of Goshen, where the children of Israel lived.

10 Plagues Of Egypt In Order:

1. Blood
2. Frogs
3. Lice or gnats
4. Flies
5. Livestock
6. Boils

7. Hail   9. Darkness
8. Locust   10. Death of firstborn

Effects Of Each Plague In More Detail:

1. Water Turned To Blood

"Thus says the Lord, 'By this you shall know that I am the Lord: behold, I will strike the water that is in the Nile with the staff that is in my hand, and it will be turned to blood. The fish that are in the Nile will die, and the Nile will become foul, and the Egyptians will find difficulty in drinking water from the Nile (Exodus 7:17-18).'"

The first plague to hit Egypt was the water of the Nile, turning to blood. The Nile River was a life source for Egypt, so this plague caused absolute disaster across the land. God used Moses and Aaron to bring this plague. He sent them to the brink of the Nile River, where Aaron raised his staff and struck the water, turning it into blood. This plague caused all the fish in the river to die and a stream of blood to flow throughout Egypt. This plague lasted for one whole week. Despite the horror, Pharaoh refused to let the Israelites go.

2. Plague Of Frogs

I will smite all your territory with frogs. So the river shall bring forth frogs abundantly, which shall go up and come into your house, into your bedroom, on your bed, into the houses of your servants, on your people, into your ovens, and into your kneading bowls. And the frogs shall come up on you, on your people, and on all your servants (Exodus 8:2-4).

The next plague involved Egypt becoming overrun by frogs. This may sound tame compared to the river of blood, but it was pretty horrific. Aaron stretched his hand out over the waters of Egypt, and frogs began to swarm throughout the land. The Bible states that frogs were everywhere, covering every piece of land in sight. Everywhere they went, the Egyptians were met with a hoard of frogs. Pharaoh couldn't believe what he saw and asked Moses and Aaron to pray to God to remove the frogs. He promised that he would let the Israelites go if the plague was gone. God removed the frogs, but Pharaoh didn't hold up his end of the deal, and the Israelites were kept in slavery.

3. Plague Of Lice Or Gnats

"So the Lord said to Moses, 'Say to Aaron, "Stretch out your rod, and strike the dust of the land, so that it may become lice throughout all the land of Egypt."' And they did so. For Aaron stretched out his hand with his rod and struck the dust of the earth, and it became lice on man and beast. All the dust of the land became lice throughout all the land of Egypt (Exodus 8:16-17)."

As Aaron struck the dust with his staff, a stream of bugs, believed to be either lice or gnats, swarmed across Egypt. The people of Egypt were tormented by these bugs, completely unable to escape them no matter where they went. Still, Pharaoh refused to let the Israelites go.

4. Plague Of Flies

"If you will not let My people go, behold, I will send swarms of flies on you and your servants, on your people and into your houses. The houses of the Egyptians shall be full of swarms of flies, and also the ground on which they stand. And in that day, I will set apart the land of Goshen, in which My people dwell, that no swarms of flies shall be there, in order that you may know that I am the Lord in the midst of the land (Exodus 8:21-22)."

The next plague continues the theme of swarming insects. After Pharaoh refused again to let God's people go free, God sent a plague of flies throughout Egypt. All of Egypt was overrun by these pesky, winged insects, except for the land of Goshen, where the Israelites lived.

5. Plague Of Livestock

Let My people go, that they may serve Me. For if you refuse to let them go, and still hold them, behold, the hand of the Lord will be on your cattle in the field, on the horses, on the donkeys, on the camels, on the oxen, and on the sheep—a very severe pestilence. And the Lord will make a difference between the livestock of Israel and the livestock of Egypt (Exodus 9:1-4).

The plague of livestock, also known as the *"plague of pestilence,"* killed all the domestic animals in Egypt. In biblical times, people's livelihoods depended on their animals, so this plague would have been particularly devastating. To add to the Egyptian's grief, they had to watch the Israelite's animals go unhurt while they dug graves for their own. Even still, Pharaoh refused to let the Israelites go.

6. Plague Of Boils

"So the Lord said to Moses and Aaron, 'Take for yourselves handfuls of ashes from a furnace, and let Moses scatter it toward the heavens in the sight of Pharaoh. And it will become fine dust in all the land of Egypt, and it will cause boils that break out in sores on man and beast throughout all the land of Egypt'" (Exodus 9:8-9).

This sixth plague is the most gruesome of all to befall Egypt—the plague of boils. This plague caused the people of Egypt to break out in awful boils all over their bodies. The pain must have been unbearable. The Egyptians were not the only ones to suffer, as the Egyptian animals were also struck with boils. The Israelites, however, were untouched.

7. Plague Of Hail

"Then the Lord said to Moses, 'Stretch out your hand toward heaven, that there may be hail in all the land of Egypt—on man, on beast, and on every herb of the field, throughout the land of Egypt.' And Moses stretched out his rod toward heaven; and the Lord sent thunder and hail, and fire darted to the ground. And the Lord rained hail on the land of Egypt (Exodus 9:22-23)."

This plague of hail hit the Egyptian people. The plague's hail was not like any that we have seen today. The Bible describes the hail that pelted down on Egypt as huge, destructive balls of ice that left no living thing unharmed. Some people were wise enough to seek shelter inside, but those who didn't were killed wherever they were. Again, the land of Goshen, where the Israelites lived, was completely untouched. This plague seemed to get through to Pharaoh, as we see in Exodus, that he sent for Moses and acknowledged his wrongdoings. For a second time, Pharaoh promised to let God's people go if the plague would stop. God stopped the hail, but Pharaoh did not set the Israelites free.

8. Plague of Locust

"if you refuse to let My people go, behold, tomorrow I will bring locusts into your territory. And they shall cover the face of the earth, so that no one will be able to see the earth; and they shall eat the residue of what is left, which remains to you from the hail, and they shall eat every tree which grows up for you out of the field (Exodus 10:4-5)."

Moses and Aaron met with Pharaoh to bargain for the Israelite's freedom, but Pharaoh would not budge. Moses warned him that even greater suffering would fall upon Egypt if he disobeyed God, but his warning fell on deaf ears. Once Moses left Pharaoh's palace, he lifted his arms to heaven, and a wind from the East brought a swarm of locusts into Egypt. It is said that the sheer volume of locusts was so much that the sun was completely blocked out. The insects forged a path of destruction across the land. Again, Pharaoh begged Moses and Aaron to pray to end the plague. Moses agreed, and God sent a wind from the west to drive the locusts away. However, once the plague was God, Pharaoh's heart hardened once again, and he refused to let the Israelites go.

9. Plague of Darkness

"Then the Lord said to Moses, 'Stretch out your hand toward heaven, that there may be darkness over the land of Egypt, darkness which may even be felt.' So Moses stretched out his hand toward heaven, and there was thick darkness in all the land of Egypt three days (Exodus 10:21-22)."

This plague cast a cloak of darkness over Egypt, which lasted several days. During this time, the Egyptians trembled in fear as no glimmer of light could be seen across the land. The Israelites continued as normal during this time in the land of Goshen, where the light remained. Darkness prompted further bargaining from Pharaoh, but he was still unwilling to offer the Israelites complete freedom. Moses left their meeting by warning Pharaoh that the final plague would be the most devastating. He informed Pharaoh that at midnight, God would pass over the land of Egypt and kill the firstborn of humans and animals. Only Israelite children would be allowed to survive this plague.

10. Plague of the Firstborn

> Then Moses said, 'Thus says the Lord: 'About midnight I will go out into the midst of Egypt; and all the firstborn in the land of Egypt shall die, from the firstborn of Pharaoh who sits on his throne, even to the firstborn of the female servant who is behind the hand mill, and all the firstborn of the animals. Then there shall be a great cry throughout all the land of Egypt, such as was not like it before, nor shall be like it again. But against none of the children of Israel shall a dog move its tongue, against man or beast, that you may know that the Lord does make a difference between the Egyptians and Israel (Exodus 11:4-7).'"

Midnight came, and, just as Moses promised, every firstborn in the land of Egypt was killed. This included the firstborn son of Pharaoh. The whole of Egypt mourned for their lost loved ones. This became known as Passover. Moses instructed the people to kill a perfect lamb and apply the lamb's blood over the doorpost and lintel of the entrance of each dwelling, effectually marking the home as believers in the protection promise from death's plague to come. This plague devastated Egypt as God used the enemy of death to persuade Pharaoh to let the Israelites go free. Pharaoh sent for Moses and Aaron that night and told the Israelites that they were free to leave Israel and take the wrath of God with them. The Israelites had been preparing for their quick exit and embarked on an exodus out of Egypt immediately.

B. LESSON: God in defeating enemies entering into Canaan Land.

God said that he would send the HORNET to drive out their enemies.

> "I will send my fear before thee and will destroy all the people to whom thou shalt come, and I will make all thine enemies turn their backs unto thee (Exodus 23:27).".

> "And I will send hornets before thee, which shall drive out the Hivite, the Canaanite, and the Hittite, from before thee (Exodus 23:28)."

> "I will not drive them out from before thee in one year; lest the land become desolate, and the beast of the field multiply against thee (Exodus 23:29)."

> "By little and little I will drive them out from before thee, until thou be increased, and inherit the land (Exodus 23:30)."

> "Moreover, the LORD thy God will send the hornet among them, until they that are left, and hide themselves from thee, be destroyed (Deuteronomy 7:20)."

The Israelites were about to enter a country occupied by idolaters, and they were commanded not to spare them or to allow them to continue in their proximity or to have any friendly relations with them. The Lord would cast out these nations and deliver them, though greater and mightier than they, into their hands; and they were to smite them and place them under the ban; they were to make no covenant with them nor form any alliances with them. Now, this act of using hornets is recorded in Joshua as he declares what God will do as they enter the Promised Land.

> "And I sent the hornet before you, which drove them out from before you, even the two kings of the Amorites; but not with thy sword, nor with thy bow (Joshua 24:12)."

God predicted He would send hornets to help drive the people out of the land (Exodus 23:28; Deuteronomy 7:20). Here He says it was fulfilled in the defeat of Sihon and Og (Numbers 21:21-35). This, no doubt, is the secret of how the Israelites took all the great giant cities of Bashan and other cities east of the Jordan.

C. LESSON: Weapons of our warfare are not carnal in nature, defeating spiritual enemies in deliverance sessions.

> "For the weapons of our warfare are not carnal, but mighty through God to the pulling down of strong holds…(2 Corinthians 10:4)."

Weapons List:
1. **Belt of TRUTH**—Ephesians 6:14.
2. **Breastplate of RIGHTEOUSNESS**—Ephesians 6:14.
3. **Shoes of the GOSPEL**—Ephesians 6:15.
4. **Shield of FAITH**—Ephesians 6:16.
5. **Helmet of SALVATION**—Ephesians 6:17.
6. **Sword of the SPIRIT**—Ephesians 6:17.
7. **Constant PRAYER**—Ephesians 6:18.
8. **Our Testimony**
9. **Battle Axe**—Jeremiah 51:20

10. Hammer of God's Word—Jeremiah 23:29
11. Fire of God
12. Binding and Loosing

D. LESSON: Defeating spiritual enemies in deliverance sessions.

To effectively defeat our spiritual enemies that take on the characteristics of their mission. When a demon takes on the persona of an entity, such as an octopus, squid, scorpion, etc., it spiritually uses the natural world enemies of such entities. In the spiritual world, you can create their reality, call their spiritual enemies to torment them and command them to leave the person going through the deliverance process.

NOTES

NOTES

NOTES

CHAPTER SEVEN

TENTACLES OF MIND CONTROL

The tentacles of Mind Control reach into the mind, will, and emotions of people. Tentacles[7] spirit "Mind Control" and the spirit "Past"

1. Tentacles are slender, flexible appendages in some invertebrates, used for feeling or grasping.

2. Tentacles are found in creatures such as the octopus and squid.

3. Mind control spirits resemble these creatures in the spirit realm and have tentacles for grasping and feeling.

4. In spiritual warfare, these tentacles need to be severed from the minds of those affected by the spirit of mind control.

5. This breaks mind control's power and speeds the deliverance.

---

7 Reference Page 238 John Eckhardt – (DSWM)

"The LORD is righteous: he hath cut asunder the cords of the wicked (Psalm 129:4)."

6. The spirit of octopus [mind control] has eight tentacles, while the squid has ten.

7. There are many interesting observations concerning mind control in culture.

8. It has been revealed that from World War II with the Vril Society techniques used to control the minds of people to commit the most horrific attacks of the minds and will of the German people, until now, mind control techniques are used to control the destiny of countries, cities, churches, and families.

9. Mind control spirits are seen in many of our images of our culture.

   a. Demonic mind control spirits are seen as octopi or squids.
   b. Octopi have eight arms.
   c. Squids have eight arms with two tentacles

10. Octopus arms are wrapped around many of our company's images or logos.

11. Octopi are seen in much of our artwork, such as an artist expressing images impressed in the spirit.

12. Mind control spirits have a beak or tooth with which they bite their prey to eat their victims.

   a. This beak is so strong it can break through bone or the prey's outer shell.

b. Many have fallen to mind control because they have not put on the helmet of salvation.

c. Some have allowed mind control to keep attacking this helmet on their head to weaken them; helmet of salvation with mind control attached.

13. Because octopi arms can regenerate if they are cut off, do not attack the tips of the arms.

a. Take the Sword of the Spirit and sever the arms at the body of the mind control octopus.

b. Anoint the front, back, and sides of a person's head with anointing oil.

c. By faith, pull the octopus tooth or beak off the top of the person's head.

d. Command mind control to loose the head of the person and come out or off.

e. Attack the mind control spirit by pulling its tooth from the top the head.

f. Some people scream while the spirit is being removed. Also, they comment there is a hole on top of their head where the tooth was previously connected.

g. Call out mind spirits as mind control comes out: mind binding, mental torment, double-mindedness, I can't remember, foggy minded, schizophrenia, dementia, memory loss, fuzzy minded, mental illness, mental block, stutter, feeble minded, dull witted, thick headed, my memory just went blank, loose screw, elevator doesn't go all the way to the top, etc.

14. An octopus has natural enemies that can be called upon to assist in removal of mind control.

a. Call for sharks and large fish to come and eat the octopus.
b. Cut off the blood to the octopus' three hearts—forbid oxygen to sustain life.
c. Octopi frequently lose an arm to predators, but they grow back.
d. Fishermen use the severed arms of octopi for bait because they continue to move after they are severed.
e. Squids and other cephalopods, such as octopi and cuttlefish, use dark ink to confuse their predators and thereby escape. The ink is contained in an ink sac, a muscular pouch beneath the gut.
f. Forbid mind control spirits to release its dark ink, not allowing this technique to distract or confuse.

15. While taking people through deliverance, many complain of headaches.

a. This is a sign that a mind control spirit is at work.
b. It is trying to stop you from proceeding in that area.
c. Remember the use of dark ink is purposed to confuse their predator.
d. Don't become distracted with the headache pain.

16. **Deliverance Session**: While addressing the candidate's migraine:

a. He was sitting in a chair in the deliverance center.
b. I told him that migraines could be caused by mind control. I asked to see if it was there.
c. I bound the spirit, cut off the tentacles, and pulled him off the top of his head. Each one of the steps were acted out to a force unseen by the natural eye, but seen in the spiritual realm.

d. Immediately, his eyes went wide eyed open, he went into a stare, and lost control of his body's ability to sit up.

e. I had to grab him to help stabilize him. He started to wretch as I called out migraine and other mental spirits.

f. After about five minutes of deliverance, he came to himself and did not remember anything that happened.

Deliverance From The Past

17. **Deliverance from The Past**[8]: Breaking the Spirit called "the Past" associated with mind control.

18. Setting a person free at this moment will keep the deliverance session from random thoughts and rabbit holes to hinder deliverance.

    a. Mind control and the Past work together. The Past will become a person's future if they continue to live in the past.

    b. Call out the Past while calling out mind control. This is why it's so important during the interview to be knowledgeable about the past.

19. Below is a testimony received as a comment a recent broadcast over the internet.
    Hi, Pastor and Greg,

    I was at your show last night [Saturday] and I believe that the spirit called "Past" came out. Never in a million years did I ever think I could be delivered ONLINE from that strong, controlling spirit I've had most of my life--but I was DETERMINED to be free and sick and tired of it!

---

8 Reference page 36, John Eckhardt - DSWM

Jesus and your online ministry did this! How cool is that! I kept sighing and cried profusely (almost wailing) and then felt extremely tired and fell asleep. I am deeply humbled and grateful for your good attitude towards helping us.

Today I can actually go to church and worship FREELY, and not be thinking about the past--I can focus on an always edifying, wonderful sermon from my good-hearted Pastor in our little country church. He's a wonderful brother in Christ, but they don't do deliverance and we all need it!

NOTES

NOTES

NOTES

CHAPTER EIGHT

LEVIATHAN

1. **Leviathan[9] is known as the king of pride and part of the marine kingdom.** He is a demonic sea creature and difficult to deliver a person. A quick reading of Job 41 says that nothing can touch him. No sword, spear, dart, habergeon, arrow, nor sling stone can cause him harm. He many times will be one of the last ones to come out as being the strongman. The lesson of Leviathan is that there are several methods to remove him from this throne of pride.

2. **Method 1: Remove Shield Demons**

   a. Leviathan will cover himself with a protective shield. The scales on his back are impenetrable and made of demons he considers strong to protect his position.

   b. This method requires you to call Leviathan to attention. Now, ask him who covers him? How many? Give the number? What are the names? I've seen coverings from 2-20+ demons.

   c. Begin by removing the shield demons one by one. Call the first demon to attention. Tell him to take the sword

---

9 Leviathan – King of Pride Reference Page 144 – 155 John Eckhardt (DSWM).

of the spirit and lift his shield off Leviathan's back. Command it to go to the pit. Repeat until all shield demons are removed. Then address the removal of Leviathan.

Leviathan and his shield Demons

© DeliveranceWithPastorHenry

3. **Method 2: Remove demons using the "one-on-one" method**

   a. This method may require more time than any other.
   b. Follow the "Deliverance Strategy—The Blue Print"
   c. Work the strategy until Leviathan is left to himself. Call him to attention, casting him to the pit.

4. **Method 3: Kilbit**

   a. There is success in causing Leviathan to suddenly leave by placing a small worm called "Kilbit" next to its gills at the deliverance candidate's neck. Threaten Leviathan with releasing a kilbit into its gills.
   b. Despite his supernatural strength, the Leviathan is afraid of this small worm that clings to the gills of large fish and kills them.

5. **Method 4: Using Spiritual Hammer**

   a. According to Job 41:24, the heart of Leviathan is hard as a stone.

      "His heart is as firm as a stone; yea, as hard as a piece of the nether millstone (Job 41:24)."

   b. According to Jeremiah 23:29 God's Word is like a hammer. Use God's hammer to crush Leviathan's stony heart.
   c. To come against him, say, "I use the hammer of God's Word to crush and break your stony heart, Leviathan. I smite your heart now. You're losing power, having a heart attack, die in the spirit." Say it over and over.

"Is not my word like as a fire? saith the LORD; and like a hammer that breaketh the rock in pieces (Jeremiah 23:29)?"

d. Pound the Bible on a surface. God strikes at the heart of Leviathan and breaks the heart of stone caused by pride.

e. Crushing the heart of pride causes him to relinquish his throne and leave.

6. Baldness: Breaking the Curse of Baldness

[16] Moreover the LORD saith, Because the daughters of Zion are haughty, and walk with stretched forth necks and wanton eyes, walking and mincing as they go, and making a tinkling with their feet: [17] Therefore the Lord will smite with a scab the crown of the head of the daughters of Zion, and the Lord will discover their secret parts. [18] In that day the Lord will take away the bravery of their tinkling ornaments about their feet, and their cauls, and their round tires like the moon, [19] The chains, and the bracelets, and the mufflers, [20] The bonnets, and the ornaments of the legs, and the headbands, and the tablets, and the earrings, [21] The rings, and nose jewels, [22] The changeable suits of apparel, and the mantles, and the wimples, and the crisping pins, [23] The glasses, and the fine linen, and the hoods, and the vails. [24] And it shall come to pass, that instead of sweet smell there shall be stink; and instead of a girdle a rent; and instead of well set hair baldness; and instead of a stomacher a girding of sackcloth; and burning instead of beauty. [25] Thy men shall fall by the sword, and thy mighty in the war. [26] And her gates shall lament and mourn; and she being desolate shall sit upon the ground (Isaiah 3:16-36).

a. There is a result for a prideful look. Verse 24 says, "Instead of well-set hair, baldness will replace the beautiful hair."

b. This is possible for all males and females, and the result of a proud look.

c. Baldness explodes in every culture from a curse of baldness because of pride.

d. Pray and break the curse of baldness over the participant. Pray restoration over the hair.

7. Burning and Stench—Verse 24

a. Look for deliverance participants who complain of burning and redness in skin tissue.

b. Look for symptoms affecting the skin caused by Leviathan:

i. Behind the ears
ii. Dryness of skin
iii. Elbows
iv. Itching
v. Rashes
vi. Sensitivity to touch areas of the skin

c. While attacking Leviathan and commanding it to come out, there may be complaints of a burning smell and stench.

d. A stench accompanying a person's body has been reported by those having Leviathan.

8. Absalom Spirit: Beauty and Baldness

a. This spirit is usually dealt with as a rebellious spirit against leadership.

"And Absalom rose up early, and stood beside the way of the gate: and it was so, that when any man that had a controversy came to the king for judgment, then Absalom called unto him, and said, Of what city art thou? And he said, Thy servant is of one of the tribes of Israel (II Samuel 15:2)."

    b. He would steal people's hearts from David by telling them if only he were the king. He would rule in their favor. He sought to bring a rebellion against the king.

2. Lesson of Absalom and Leviathan, as the king of all the children of pride.

    c. Absalom was the third son of David, king of Israel. There was none to be praised for his beauty above Absalom. There was no blemish in him.

"But in all Israel, there was none to be so much praised as Absalom for his beauty: from the sole of his foot even to the crown of his head there was no blemish in him. 26 And when he polled his head, (for it was at every years end that he polled *it:* because *the hair* was heavy on him, therefore he polled it:) he weighed the hair of his head at two hundred shekels after the king's weight.

    d. The Bible says Absalom was praised as the most handsome man in all Israel: "He was flawless from head to foot." When he cut his hair once a year—only because it became too heavy—it weighed five pounds. It seemed everyone loved him.

    e. Absalom had a beautiful sister named Tamar, who was a virgin. Another of David's sons, Amnon, was their half-brother. Amnon fell in love with Tamar, raped her, then rejected her in disgrace.

    f. For two years, Absalom kept silent, sheltering Tamar in his home. He had expected his father, David, to punish

Amnon for his act. When David did nothing, Absalom's rage and anger seethed into a vengeful plot.

g. One day, Absalom invited all the king's sons to a sheep-shearing festival. While Amnon was celebrating, Absalom ordered his soldiers to kill him.

h. After the assassination, Absalom fled to Geshur, northeast of the Sea of Galilee, to the house of his grandfather. He hid there for three years. David missed his son deeply. The Bible says in II Samuel 13:37 that David "mourned for his son day after day." Finally, David allowed him to come back to Jerusalem.

i. Gradually, Absalom began to undermine King David, usurping his authority and speaking against him. Under the pretense of honoring a vow, Absalom went to Hebron and began to gather an army. He sent messengers throughout the land, proclaiming his kingship.

j. When King David learned of the rebellion, he and his followers fled Jerusalem. Meanwhile, Absalom took advice from his counselors on the best way to defeat his father. Before the battle, David ordered his troops to not harm Absalom. The two armies clashed at Ephraim, in a large oak forest. Twenty thousand men fell that day. David's army prevailed.

k. As Absalom was riding his mule under a tree, his hair entangled in the branches. The mule ran off, leaving Absalom hanging in the air, helpless. Joab, one of David's generals, took three javelins and thrust them into Absalom's heart. Then ten of Joab's armor-bearers circled Absalom and killed him.

l. Here is the lesson: Absalom was a rebellious murderer. He killed his brother and then purposed to steal the kingdom from David.

m. The story began and it ended with his hair. Absalom's hair was his downfall. He was prideful about his looks and hair.

n. As I was taking a woman through deliverance and at the point of identifying Leviathan's shield demons, he gave the name of Absalom as a shield demon. As I was looking at this female, I saw here beautiful black, long, curly hair.

o. I said to her, "I would say you get a lot of complements about how pretty your hair is." When I said that, she took both her hands and started lifting her hair, turning her head in a provocative way.

p. She replied, "Yes," she did. She said that was one reason she sought me for deliverance because her hair was falling out and balding.

q. If we had not interrogated Leviathan about the shield demons on his back, in the natural, we would not have found this balding demon attacking her.

r. Call out this spirit any time you are calling out Leviathan. This spirit of Absalom causes baldness and rebellion. In this case, baldness must be dealt with.

3. Leviathan Can Be Represented As A Four-Square City

a. Look for a square balding patch on top of the head. Arba (Joshua 14:15)

b. Arba means "city of four giants." The name of a giant meaning "a cube, strength, or four-sided square."

c. "And the name of Hebron before was Kirjatharba; which Arba was a great man among the Anakims. And the land had rest from war (Joshua 14:15)."

d. A symbol of great strength and stability; characterized in the cube square; Kirjatharba, which means "the city of giants."

e. Judges 1:10 states, "And Judah went against the Canaanites that dwelt in Hebron: (now the name of Hebron before was Kirjatharba:) and they slew Sheshai, and Ahiman, and Talmai."

f. Deliverance Lesson: While preparing to take a man through deliverance, I noticed a balding square on top of his head. The Holy Spirit directed me to Arba, the four-side square city of giants. While calling up Leviathan, he responded he had four shield demons. Start the process of calling up the shied demons. The shield demon said it was part of the city of giants, Arba.

g. Beware of this on the top of a person's head, male or female. This has been seen on the top of both genders.

4. **Manifestation of Leviathan:** Twisting in the back, pain in the back, curved spine.

a. Leviathan will twist parts of the body as it manifests coming out.

b. Many have twisted backs, jaws, necks, and curved spines.

c. Torment of pain in the back, pain in lower spine, and all with unknown causes. Remove this demonic stronghold and remove the torment of pain.

d. Scoliosis known as curvature of the spine is cause by this spirit of Leviathan.

NOTES

NOTES

NOTES

CHAPTER NINE

LEVIATHAN'S SHIELD DEMONS

The process of identifying Leviathan's shield demons is the key to the removal of this strongman.

Shield Demons

1. Follow the procedure provided to remove Leviathan, a strongman whose armor must be removed. Removing his armor [shield demons] is required before casting out Leviathan.

2. His shield demons cause a person to hold on to their pride, which supports Leviathan.

3. These demons have linked themselves together to protect themselves and Leviathan.

   "One is so near to another, that no air can come between them (Job 41:16)."

4. You must identify each shield and strip the shield demons off his back. It is easy to be fooled by Leviathan because he doesn't want to lose his throne of pride. Never underestimate a person oppressed by pride.

Follow this process of identifying the shield demons:

Step 1. Call up Leviathan and interrogate him. How many shield demons cover his back? Record that number.

Step 2. Interrogate Leviathan. Who is in the number one position on his back? Record the names and move to the next one. After all the names are recorded, command Leviathan to go down.

Step 3. Call up Shield demon number one. Ask the evil spirit, "What is your mission?" Record this mission. This is important to the person to help them fight the battle when the spirit tries to come back.

Step 4. Once all the shield demons are removed. Call up Leviathan and remove him.

5. The mission of each shield demon is very important to share with the candidate post-deliverance.

6. The Scriptures tell us that once a demon has left his house, after a time, he will try to return.

"When the unclean spirit is gone out of a man, he walketh through dry places, seeking rest; and finding none, he saith, I will return unto my house whence I came out. **25** And when he cometh, he findeth it swept and garnished. **26** Then goeth he, and taketh *to him* seven other spirits more wicked than himself; and they enter in, and dwell there: and the last *state* of that man is worse than the first (Luke 11:24-26)."

7. Leviathan is not coming back with a small demon. He will bring back his shield demons and more.

8. Bringing seven more wicked than himself is because he lost his throne of pride by using these shields, therefore he will reinforce himself with stronger ones.

9. **Shield Example**: A 75-year-old male professional boxer involved with multiple marriages is now married to a 65-year-old woman. He has many sexual dreams and earnestly wants deliverance. He gave 10 shield demons:

   a. Kitty Kat—sex with women's parts of their bodies

   b. Hercules—loves boxing

   c. Fatigue—tired of working

   d. Parachute- doubt and unbelief, would trust God for steps of faith

   e. Huckleberry—ready to fight

   f. Raisin—concerned about what his face looks like

   g. Heaven—fear of heights

   h. Great—considerably better than anyone else

i. Coffee—I want to have sex with you (spirit spouse(s)—star and sun)

j. Pain—back Pain is a ten

10. **Shield Example**: A 35-year-old man was in prison nine years. He came for deliverance, and there were seven shield demons on Leviathan's back.

    1. Cloudy Mind—life, makes bad decisions

    2. I am a Liar—lie to his wife where he was at, she was concerned that he was selling drugs.

    3. Drugs—makes him sell drugs for money.

    4. Revenge—seeks revenge for someone who killed his cousin.

    5. Guilt—destroy his life, steal his peace.

    6. Unworthy—to be a husband or loved.

    7. Fear—makes him loose sleep at night, paranoia.

11. **Shield Example**: Alex, a 50-year-old man with two shield demons: intellectualism and resilience.

12. **Leviathan**: King of Pride Page 144–155 John Eckhardt (DSWM).

NOTES

NOTES

NOTES

Deeper Deliverance and Discernment

CHAPTER TEN

SPIRIT SPOUSES

Incubus and Succubus

The spirit spouse is a sexual spirit that torments individuals and married couples.

Video Comment: From the video "Spirit Spouse on Deliverance with Pastor Henry" 9/2022

Thank you, Pastor Henry, for that. It was awesome. I cough, burp, yawn, and vomit. I was watching a zoom video and heard audibly in my left ear, "I am not coming out," because I know it is an incubus. Sometimes I feel something in my private area. I am divorced. He was in adultery, so I think it came from that. Thank you! I have been doing self-deliverance for some time, but you need somebody anointed for this.

1. I receive emails, phone calls, and texts globally from spouses asking about spirit spouses, seeking help. In the grand scheme, few ministers are helping God's people.

Spirit Spouse with Soul Ties

© DeliveranceWithPastorHenry

2. **Spirit Spouse**: Incubus, Succubus, Lilith

   a. The Incubus is a male spirit who normally attacks a female.
   b. The Succubus is a female spirit who attacks the male.
   c. A spirit spouse is a demonic spirit that attaches itself to a person. It claims this person as their own property. In a sense, it will "marry" a person.
   d. The spirit spouse can be male or female.

94

3. A person can have multiple spirit spouses.

4. The encounter may come as a person is approaching twilight sleep, REM sleep, or while reawaking. There will be a sense of sexual gratification, sexual release, and ejaculation.

5. Moreover, the sexual molestation can continue in a fully awake mind. Even while sitting, standing, or lying down, the attack can be constant or intermittent.

6. A spirit spouse may cause sexual dreams with a person or itself. Masturbation is possible during sleep as this spirit is controlling them.

7. Often, the spirit will take the name of the deceased husband or wife, masking as the deceased partner or familiar person.

8. A spirit spouse can be malevolent toward the human. It has been reported that when a female said "No," and pushed away the spirit, it became violent and attacked her.

9. Call up the spirit spouse, ask its name, and how many spirit spouses there are.

10. Have the person renounce the spirit spouse by divorcing them in the spirit realm.

11. Act out reaching to married ring finger, pulling off a ring, and tossing it away. Saying, "I divorce you in the spirit realm, and declare a divorce."

12. Then, call out the spirit and command it to go to the pit.

13. Lilith: The Seducer

The name Lilith stems from lilû, lilîtu, and (w)ardat lilî). The Akkadian word lilu is related to the Hebrew **word lilith in Isaiah 34:14**, which is thought to be a night bird by some modern scholars such as Judit M. Blair.[6] **In the** Ancient Mesopotamian religion, found in cuneiform **texts of** Sumer, Assyria, and Babylonia **Lilith signifies a spirit or demon.**

14. Incubus and Succubus are evil spirits that lay on top of an individual during sleep, especially having sexual intercourse with an individual while sleeping. These spirits oppress or burden a person, such as a nightmare.

15. Incubus attacks females, while Succubus attacks males. These spirits operate through witchcraft spells, sexual sin, perversion, and curses of lust [whoredom]. They are filthy spirits causing lustful dreams followed by tormenting the individual with guilt and condemnation.

Eckhardt, John. Deliverance and Spiritual Warfare Manual (p. 225). Charisma House. Kindle Edition.

16. A woman reported sleeping in her mother-in-law's bedroom when she was attacked by a spirit spouse sexual demon.

17. Look for "Marriage Ceremony" of a spirit spouse claiming to be a familiar person in a dream.

18. Sexual petting, kissing, or fondling can open a door to spirit spouse oppression.

19. In many cultures, a Shaman is expected to have a spirit spouse as a rite of office.

20. Religious nuns report having become the bride of Jesus with a sexual encounter.

A Request for Deliverance, as received:

I have been watching on Deep Believer, YouTube Channel, I have listened to the program and the first time I heard of Pastor Henry Shaffer. I've watched the program over and over many times I have delivered from many evil spirits. With the Lilith spirit spouse, I followed what Pastor Henry said to do and it worked, my actions line up with his words as he spoke, I did what he said. I have been set free and I feel so happy it have changed my innermost spirit I am so grateful that this has helped me I feel like a new person even deliverance from Pharaoh spirit. I feel like I have been set free accept as he spoke of the octopus and squid spirit I was feeling good then my head started hurting not with sharp pains just an ache in my head which covered my head enough to let me know it was there and after that it would go away for a little bit and come right back. I don't have headaches ever I did but he said on TV and that pain left me, but I do wonder as he describes the leviathan spirit that may be one in me. I heard a voice from inside of me. I'm the last on left as I was wonder about that I don't know if it's my wrong thinking or if I have that spirit. I don't know. I do know I have been set free like a bird out of a cage. I felt the spirits as they came out, I coughed them out much I want to thank Pastor Henry Shaffer. I needed him I needed his help. I'm a 70-year-old woman I'm a widow who lives alone. The Spirit Spouse after I ask said the name Augusta under Pastor Henry Shaffer words was cast out of me. I dreamed I was married but it was an odd dream. I just got married; I was standing in a white dress. I could not see the bottom of this dress there was an arrangement of feathers like a hat, and I could see that on my head it was pretty white. My wedding gown was a pretty white lacy top but my husband was nowhere to be found. I couldn't see him or no one else but I knew I was married. I looked up the name Augusta, is the female name from the male name Augustus which proclaim to be a God in the Bible. The birth stone as I looked it up Augusta or Augustus has two colors one is a green the other is red not apple red but red with the word spine. My father, when I was a child, was not nice to any of us I would sit down beside my father on the side sofa he would put his hands down with the palm of his hand up so when I set down my 4, 5, or 6-year-old bottom was on his hand. I learned not to do that. This spirit spouse would start his touch on me from the bottom of my spine just like my father who had a bad drinking problem. There was a ring I received many years ago I don't know if this is important. I was going to a yard sale I stop my car in her yard a woman walked up to me right then she had a ring she said she just found it in the yard is what she said an she gave it to me with me asking her don't you want to keep it she said no it's a pretty red ring the same color of the birth stone Augusta or Augustus I still have it. I am throwing it away I believe I still need help would you pray for me. I believe I still need help. I've not be faithful in my walk with God, at one point I turned my back on God it was horrible for me. I never want to do that again I am grateful God has received me back. Please pray for me churches here they don't ever mention deliverance of demons. They don't mention hardly anything about his soon coming. I have learned more from the preachers on TV. Thank you for reading this.

NOTES

NOTES

NOTES

CHAPTER ELEVEN

PAN

A Spirit Spouse is a sexual spirit that torments individual persons and marriage couples.

1. **Pan:** god over masturbation

2. To further complete the deliverance process from the spirit husbands or wives, it is necessary to remove the deepest of sexual entities of Satan's kingdom, Pan.

3. Many continue to struggle with the torment of spirit husbands and spirit wives.

4. God answering my prayer of petition wanting to know why he had no freedom. He said, "You aren't getting to the root of their problem."

5. **Sexual Sins:** Listed below are areas identified as demons to cast out. It is as a guideline for deliverance from sexual sins. This is a normal list of sins with demons attached:

   a. Bestiality

   b. Fornication

   c. Homosexuality

   d. Incest

e. Lust
f. Masturbation
g. Molestation
h. Pornography

i. Rape
j. Sexual abuse of others
k. Sexual dreams

6. Having to go deeper and freeing people from spirit spouses is a difficult deliverance. Many fail to get to the root, and others fail because of the spirit's sexual nature.

7. Demons know culture and history. They mask themselves with truth and fables. Learn from the past and you can know the revelation secret of how the demons will hide in view of someone's bondage.

8. In Greek religion and mythology, Pan (/'pæn/; Ancient Greek: Πάν, Pan) is the god of the wild, shepherds and flocks, nature of mountain wilds, hunting and rustic music, and companion of the nymphs.

9. His name originates within the Ancient Greek language, from the word paein (πάειν), meaning "to pasture."

10. Pan has the hindquarters, legs, and horns of a goat, in the same manner as a faun or satyr. With his homeland in rustic Arcadia, he is also recognized as the god of fields, groves, and wooded glens. Because of this, Pan is connected to fertility and the season of spring.

11. **History**: The parentage of Pan is unclear. Generally, he is considered the son of Hermes, although in some myths he is the son of Zeus, or Dionysus, with whom his mother is said to be a nymph.

12. **All Sexual Partners**: Some myths reflect the folk etymology that equates Pan's name (Πάν) with the Greek word for "all" (πᾶν), because of the many sexual partners his mother supposedly had.

13. **Worship**: The worship of Pan began in Arcadia, which was always the principal seat of his worship. These are often referred to as the "Cave of Pan."

14. **Orgies:** where men and women would face each other, then visually sexually stimulate each other was often the norm. As the participants climaxed, there would be deep guttural sounds made from within.

15. One of the famous myths of Pan involves the origin of his pan flute, fashioned from lengths of hollow reed. Syrinx was a lovely water-nymph of Arcadia.

16. As she was returning from the hunt one day, Pan met her. To escape his importunities, the fair nymph ran away and didn't stop to hear his compliments. He pursued her until she came to her sisters, who immediately changed her into a reed.

17. When the air blew through the reeds, it produced a plaintive melody. The god, still infatuated, took some of the reeds because he could not identify which reed she became. He cut seven pieces—or according to some versions, nine, joined them side by side gradually decreasing lengths, and formed the musical instrument bearing the name of his beloved Syrinx. Henceforth, Pan was seldom seen without it.

18. **Erotic Aspects of Masturbation**: Because Pan was considered so painfully ugly, he could not seem to seduce

partners. Therefore, Pan was given the secret of learning masturbation from his father, Hermes, and teaching the habit to shepherds.

19. **Panic**: Disturbed in his secluded afternoon naps, Pan's angry shout inspired panic in lonely places. Following the Titans' assault on Olympus, Pan claimed credit for the victory of the gods because he had frightened the attackers. In the Battle of Marathon (490 BC), it is said that Pan favored the Athenians and so inspired panic in the hearts of their enemies, the Persians.

20. **Deception**: Pan's greatest conquest was that of the moon goddess, Selene. He accomplished this by wrapping himself in a sheepskin to hide his hairy black goat form and drew her down from the sky into the forest where he seduced her.

a. Pan will appear in your dreams as someone familiar to you.
b. He wants you to open the door to him in dreams.
c. Pan will appear as a male or female, satyr, or animal in a dream state to confuse you in a sexual encounter in a dream resulting in a "wet dream."

21. **All the Pans**: Pan could be multiplied into a swarm of Pans. Myths where the god Pan had twelve sons that helped Dionysus in his war against the Indians.

22. **Look for Multiples of Pan**: Their names were: (reference only)

a. Aigikoros
b. Argennon
c. Argos
d. Daphoineus
e. Eugeneios
f. Glaukos
g. Kelaineus
h. Omester

i. Philamnos k. Phorbas
j. Phobos l. Xanthos

23. Pan will work with the spirit spouses to cause masturbation during twilight sleep. He can infiltrate dreams with his presence, masked as a spirit spouse, someone of known origin, or even a stranger. He hopes to engage you by deception, therefore opening avenues of oppression.

24. Prepped by the Lord, God sent a man, a pastor having a problem at night. His wife reported she was afraid to sleep with him because of the strange manifestation happening at night in him while lying next to him in bed—items falling off the wall and waking up startled.

25. Strange voices come out of him, and his back seems to be moving and bulging.

26. **Deliverance Summary:**

   a. I contacted them and set aside time in my schedule to help.
   b. They drove five hours to get to the deliverance session after informing them of having the torment of spirit spouses.
   c. By a word of knowledge, I told the pastor his problem was caused by a spirit called Pan.
   d. He said that is the one with goat's feet and a man's body and it chases him in dreams.
   e. He has my parents chained to a tree wearing an orange jump suit.
   f. I didn't know Pan was the one chasing him in his dreams, but God did.

g. The deliverance went according to the outline discussed in this book.

h. We revealed the first shield demon on Leviathan's back as Pan.

i. The pastor got tremendously ill and insisted the deliverance session come to an end.

j. His wife was distraught over his decision to quit.

k. Pan was very strong in this pastor.

l. The bottom line is that the pastor's wife was so scared of what she saw in the bedroom and heard come from the pastor that she sought deliverance, but he did not.

m. She received deliverance, most definitely. She asked if she was supposed to take home the demon left in the pastor.

n. "Yes, and you need to bind it every night before bedtime," I replied.

o. Also, I informed her if she could convince him to come back, they would be worked into the schedule for deliverance.

27. Hidden deeper than spirits of masturbation is the god over masturbation, the spirit Pan.

28. God delivers us from our enemies, not our friends.

29. The strange noises heard from the pastor's bedroom at night were caused by Pan, who wants to instill panic.

30. See Pan's mode of operation equaling panic to torment you.

31. I've received reports that fire alarms have gone off in the middle of the night with no explanation from professional installers and maintenance persons over fire alarm systems.

32. While the deliverance process can be lengthy, this area is one to give attention to details.

33. Look for multiple spirit spouses, masturbation, and Pans.

34. Symptoms of panic without normal causes, during sleeping with wife or husband to disturb their sleep to get them afraid to be together.

35. Spirit of Pan will manifest with the person, grabbing their private areas and imitating sexual acts.

36. Articles are written by many pastors saying they can't believe in spirit spouses[10]. Doubt and unbelief are bars in the prison walls.

---

10 Link to Article: https://africa.thegospelcoalition.org/article/why-i-cant-be-lieve-in-spirit-husbands-and-spirit-wives/

NOTES

NOTES

NOTES

CHAPTER TWELVE

PHARAOH

Pharaoh stands between a person and their deliverance.

1. Pharaoh[11] is the title given to ancient Egyptian rulers. Pharaoh is also used as a proper noun in the Bible. Today, referring to someone as a pharaoh means he is a tyrant. The adjective form is pharaonic. Pharaoh comes from the Egyptian pr-'o, which means great house.

2. **Lesson:** This strongman spirit will stunt church and people's growth. It will not free God's people. He keeps them from their spiritual progress in bondage.

3. In Egyptian society, religion **was central to everyday life. One of the roles of** Pharaoh was as an intermediary between the deities and people. Pharaoh thus deputized for the deities in a role both as civil and religious administrator.

4. **Lukewarmness:** the taskmaster used to keep people from seeing the necessity of deliverance.

---

11 Pharaoh Spirit - Page 126 John Eckhardt (DSWM) adapted.

5. **Procrastination:** putting off tasks until later is a sign that pharaoh with lukewarmness is at work.

6. **Taskmasters:** These demons are called taskmasters assigned to hinder and impede your spiritual walk.

7. **Bricks without straw:** These are spirits of poverty and indebtedness, assigned to keep you poor and always depending on government handouts. Living on the dole of the government for generations is its assignment.

8. **Jannes and Jambres:** the bewitching of pharaoh, the power arm of the occult at work in a person's life. Break the occult involvement in generational curses.

   "And Moses **and** Aaron **went in unto** Pharaoh, and they did so as the LORD **had commanded: and Aaron cast down his** rod **before Pharaoh, and before his** servants, and it became a serpent. Then Pharaoh also called the wise men and the sorcerers: now the magicians **of Egypt, they also did in like manner with their** enchantments. For they cast down every man his rod, and they became serpents: but Aaron's rod swallowed up their rods (Exodus 7:10-12).

   "Now as Jannes and Jambres withstood Moses, so do these also resist the truth: men of corrupt minds, reprobate concerning the faith (II Timothy 3:8)."

9. Attack and cast out these demonic spirits while calling out pharaoh and lukewarmness.

   a. Angel of Death
   b. Boils and Blains

   c. Crocodile—Dragon
      Serpent Spirits

d. Darkness three days—blind leading blind

e. Death of the First-born of men and cattle

f. Egypt—Spirit of Egypt

g. Fear of Leaving Egypt

h. Hail mixed with Fire—fire of judgment

i. Heaviness - Depression

j. Jambres—name meaning Poverty, bitter, a rebel

k. Jannes—name meaning Seduce or Cheat

l. Judgment of Frogs against you

m. Judgment of water to blood against you

n. Laodicea—I'm in no need of anything

o. Lice—gnats against you— Distraction

p. Locusts—no money

q. Pestilence of live-stock—worries of worldly things

r. Sorcery

s. Speak judgment over Pharaoh—the plagues of Egypt against Pharaoh Spirit

t. The one that says," make bricks without straw." (This is poverty and indebtedness)

u. Tyrant

v. Wild animals—Flies

NOTES

NOTES

NOTES

CHAPTER THIRTEEN

LUKEWARMNESS

Lukewarmness and Pharaoh spirit work together to keep a person in bondage.

1. Lukewarmness is the taskmaster used to keep people from seeing the necessity of deliverance.

> And unto the angel of the church of the Laodiceans write; These things saith the Amen, the faithful and true witness, the beginning of the creation of God; ¹⁵ I know thy works, that thou art neither cold nor hot: I would thou wert cold or hot. ¹⁶ So then because thou art lukewarm, and neither cold nor hot, I will spue thee out of my mouth. ¹⁷ Because thou sayest, I am rich, and increased with goods, and have need of nothing; and knowest not that thou art wretched, and miserable, and poor, and blind, and naked: ¹⁸ I counsel thee to buy of me gold tried in the fire, that thou mayest be rich; and white raiment, that thou mayest be clothed, and that the shame of thy nakedness do not appear; and anoint thine eyes with eye salve, that thou mayest see. ¹⁹ As many as I love, I rebuke and chasten: be zealous therefore, and repent (Revelation 3:14-19).

2. **Setup:** You're in captivity | lukewarmness | pharaoh | your deliverance | destiny.

3. Pharaoh uses lukewarmness to convince pastors, churches, or Christians that there is no need for deliverance. It says, "You don't have a lukewarm spirit," but you really know there is a problem.

4. In many cases, as the spirit of lukewarmness is called out, when this spirit manifests, many report their entire body getting hot, their hands or feet warm significantly, and their body rises in temperature.

5. Lukewarmness is a marine spirit and is revealed in Revelation 3 as the source of water consumption to Laodicea.

6. When this spirit is called out, many report their bodies warming as it manifests and comes out. Feet and hands may start to warm. Look for signs of this manifestation.

NOTES

NOTES

NOTES

CHAPTER FOURTEEN

PANDEMIC DELIVERANCE

The recent pandemic brought a demonic attack on the Body of Christ that the world has not seen before. The Church is affected by Demons of death and sickness because of this pandemic.

1. The COVID-19 virus attacks human bodies and originated from China. The spiritual root involves symbolism from China and the virus' host.

2. Many have reported that snakes must play in this spiritual and physical attack.

3. People have complained of the lingering COVID-19 effects.

4. Some express their lungs are burning like fire as the COVID-19 spirit is called out. Have them breathe slowly, or if they are coughing, command it to come out in Jesus' name.

5. Have the deliverance participant renounce any unforgiveness. Break word curses spoken over them concerning COVID-19. Follow the list to expel unwanted spirits of demonic activity or linger lingering affects of:

a. Boa Constrictor
b. China Virus
c. Cobra
d. Death
e. I can't breathe
f. Johnson and Johnson
g. King Cobra
h. Modena
i. Pfizer

j. Premature death
k. Python
l. Red Dragon
m. Restricted breathing
n. Serpent
o. Shortness of breath
p. Suffocation in the lungs

6. Lingering effects of COVID-19 are called "long haulers." These spirits cause unwanted symptoms to linger after a person recovered from the initial onset of this virus.

a. Blood flow disorder
b. Brain Damage
c. Fatigue
d. Foggy Minded
e. Follow the list below to expel the demons.
f. Heart Damage
g. Itching patch skin

h. Kidney Damage
i. Loss of Smell
j. Loss of Taste
k. Memory Loss
l. Other organ damage
m. Spirit that causes Baldness
n. Whelps

7. COVID-19 Syndrome[12]

a. COVID-19 biological attack on the world. Released from Wuhan, China.
b. Caused much devastation to the world's economy, personal health, and many global deaths.

---

12 https://www.mayoclinic.org/diseases-conditions/coronavirus/in-depth/coronavirus-long-term-effects/art-20490351

8. What are the symptoms of post-COVID-19 syndrome? The most reported symptoms of post-COVID-19 syndrome include:

   a. Fatigue
   b. Fever
   c. Lung [respiratory] symptoms, including difficulty breathing or shortness of breath and cough.
   d. Symptoms that get worse after physical or mental effort

9. Other possible symptoms include:

   a. Neurological symptoms or mental health conditions, including difficulty thinking or concentrating, headache, sleep problems, dizziness when standing, pins-and-needles feeling, loss of smell or taste, and depression or anxiety.
   b. Joint or muscle pain
   c. Heart symptoms or conditions, including chest pain and fast or pounding heartbeat.
   d. Digestive symptoms, including diarrhea and stomach pain.
   e. Blood clots and blood vessel [vascular] issues, including a blood clot that travels to the lungs from deep veins in the legs and blocks blood flow to the lungs (pulmonary embolism)
   f. Other symptoms, such as a rash and changes in the menstrual cycle

10. Keep in mind that it can be hard to tell if you are having symptoms due to COVID-19 or another cause, such as a preexisting medical condition.

11. It's also not clear if post-COVID-19 syndrome is new and unique to COVID-19. Some symptoms are like those caused by chronic fatigue syndrome and other chronic illnesses that develop after infections. Chronic fatigue syndrome involves extreme fatigue that worsens with physical or mental activity but doesn't improve with rest.

12. Why does COVID-19 cause ongoing health problems?

13. Organ damage could play a role. People who had severe illness with COVID-19 might experience organ damage affecting the heart, kidneys, skin and brain.

14. If you see someone who needs help, reference:

    a. Doctor Bryan Ardis
    b. Doctor and Show Host, Founder and CEO Ardis Labs
    c. Web Address is https://www.drardisshow.com

NOTES

NOTES

NOTES

CHAPTER FIFTEEN

SATANIC RITUALLY ABUSED

1. Satanic ritual abuse (SRA) or ritual abuse may be defined as a control method over people of all ages consisting of physical, sexual, and psychological mistreatment using rituals, with or without satanic meaning or overtones. Perpetrators of SRA may utilize satanic rituals as part of their belief system and/or to facilitate the control and mistreatment of their victims.

2. Start the deliverance process with the individual by doing an extensive interview.

3. Let them express their life story. You must listen and take copious notes.

4. There is a strategy of deliverance. Follow the five steps in the Strategy section.

   a. Bitterness
   b. Leviathan
   c. Mind Control
   d. Shield Demons
   e. Stubbornness
   f. Unforgiveness

5. This process will expose fractures, multiples, fragmented memories.

6. **"Voices" spirit:** Check for this spirit.

    a. Call it up.
    b. Ask, "Are you there?"
    c. How many voices?
    d. What are the names of each voice?
    e. Record and start the removal process.

7. Additional Reference Russ Dizdar—The Black Awakening

NOTES

NOTES

NOTES

CHAPTER SIXTEEN

SIGNS OF DEMON DELIVERANCE

1. When demonic spirits depart, look for one of the signs of deliverance.

2. If there is no manifestation as listed below, there isn't any deliverance. In other words, no demon has been cast out. The spirit remains in the person.

3. Signs of deliverance from demonic spirits are listed below:

   a. Belching—Burping
   b. Blowing Nose
   c. Coughing
   d. Crying
   e. Drooling
   f. Eyes—cool breeze flowing from eyes
   g. Hiccups
   h. Laughing
   i. Passing Gas
   j. Pressure/Air escaping ears
   k. Retching
   l. Roaring
   m. Screaming
   n. Sneezing
   o. Sweating
   p. Vomiting
   q. Whistling
   r. Yawning

NOTES

NOTES

NOTES

SECTION III

Documents Links Miscellaneous

ADULT PERSONAL HINDRANCE INVENTORY— DOCUMENT 001 FRONT

Possessiveness	Sexual	Anger Issues
a. Gambling	a. Adultery	a. Aggressiveness (toward others)
b. Greed	b. Fornication	b. Bitterness
c. Hoarding	c. Homosexuality	c. Hatred
d. Indebtedness	d. Incest	d. Murder
e. Jealousy	e. Lust	e. Rage
f. Laziness	f. Masturbation	f. Revenge
g. Poverty	g. Molestation	g. Temper
h. Stealing	h. Pornography	h. Temper tantrums
i. Stinginess	i. Rape	i. Unwilling to forgive
	j. Sexual Abuse of others	j. Violence

Fears	Addictions	Rebellion (Toward God/ Authority)
a. Anxiety (w/o known threat)	(name)	
b. Fear of closed places	a. Alcohol	a. Arrogance
c. Fear of evil or demons	b. Anorexia	b. Controlling attitude
d. Fear of failure	c. Bulimia	c. Disobedience
e. Fear of heights	d. Caffeine	d. Lawlessness
f. Fear of losing salvation	e. Illegal drugs	e. Pride
g. Fear of man	f. Overeating	f. Stubbornness
h. Fear of the dark	g. Prescription Medications	g. Witchcraft
i. Fear of the unknown		
j. Panic attacks		

NOTES

NOTES

ADULT PERSONAL HINDRANCE INVENTORY: DOCUMENT-001 BACK

Occult Involvement (addicted to)	Uncontrolled Tongue	False Religions
a. Bloody Mary	a. Exaggeration	a. Bahaism
b. Consulting psychics	b. Foul mouth denial	b. Buddhism
c. E.S.P.	c. Gossip	c. Cults
d. Fortune telling	d. Lying	d. Eastern Religions
e. Free Masonry	e. Pathological Lying	e. Indian Religions
f. Horoscope	f. Slander Cursing	f. Islam
g. Horror Movies		g. Jehovah Witnesses
h. Hypnotism		h. Mormonism
i. Meditation		i. Unity, etc.
j. Ouija board		j. Other
k. Palm reading		
l. Satanism	**Physical Diseases**	**Mental Illness**
m. Séances		
n. Spirit Guide	a. Autoimmune disease	a. ADD and ADHD
o. Tarot Cards	b. Cancer	b. Autistic disorders
p. Voodoo	c. Diabetes	c. Bipolar disorders
q. Water witching	d. Heart disease	d. Narcissism
r. Witchcraft	e. Kidney stones	e. Obsessive compulsive
s. Yoga	f. Lung disease	f. Personality disorders
	g. Migraine headaches	g. Schizophrenia
	h. Received Blood	h. Other
	i. Received Organ Transfusion	
	j. Transplant	
	k. Other	

Note: This is a sample of demonic spirits listed by category. As you explore in the deliverance sessions you can add to this listing.

NOTES

NOTES

DELIVERANCE INTERVIEW LIFE DATA SHEET— DOCUMENT-002

Name: _____

Date: _____

NOTES

NOTES

PREPARING FOR DELIVERANCE SESSION: DELIVERANCE GUIDELINES DOCUMENT-003

Step 1. Preparing a person for deliverance, follow this guideline:

1. Bind the strong man.
2. Forbid any retaliation (those present, family, pets, friends etc.)
3. Forbid any rending or tearing of the body.
4. Forbid spirits to transfer from candidate to deliverance team members.
5. Break all generational curses.
6. Break all soul ties.

Step 2. Dealing with witchcraft background in every deliverance candidate:

1. Break all blood covenants.
2. Break all dedications.
   a. all male children
   b. all female children
   c. all first born
3. Blind the third eye using anointing oil by placing a symbolic cross on the forehead.

Step 3. Setting someone free from occult activities and/or oppression always:

1. Bind all witches covens in the area trying to prevent deliverance sessions.
2. Speak destruction over Satan's altar circle and all implements performed by witches.
3. Cut off all transfer spirits, i.e., forbid astral-projection in to or from the area.

Step 4. Breaking a curse over an individual or family bloodline:

1. Ask the Lord for forgiveness of sins.
2. Ask the Lord for forgiveness of ancestor's sins on both sides of the family as far back as necessary.
3. Put those sins under the blood of Jesus (person's and ancestor's sins).
4. Close all open doors, known or unknown.
5. Ask the Lord to break any ungodly soul ties with family and/ or others. Name the person if possible.

6. Ask the Lord to lift the curse from the individual being delivered and his/her family to prevent it from continuing down the bloodline.
7. Bind activities each day of curses.

Step 5. Protection Prayer

1. **Before Starting:** I call for the Lord's angels to surround you and cover you and everyone present with Jesus' blood.
2. I draw a bloodline between you and each of us.
3. I bind your hands and feet with the threefold cord of Ecclesiastes 4:12 and you will remain in that chair.

Step 6. Forgiveness Prayer

1. Have deliverance candidate repeat this prayer of forgiveness:

   "Father God, others have trespassed against me, but in obedience to Your command I now forgive each person who has ever hurt me in any way. As an act of my will, I now forgive (name them, both living and dead), in Jesus' name."

2. Father God, I bless each of these individuals. I love them with Your love, and I ask You to forgive them also. And since You have forgiven me, I also forgive myself and accept myself in the name of Jesus Christ. The curse of unforgiveness has no more power in my life. Amen.

NOTES

NOTES

CHILDREN PERSONAL HINDRANCE INVENTORY

Emotional	Occult Involvement	Disorders
a. Abandonment		a. ADD/ADHD
b. Bipolar Disorder	a. Devil	b. Arrested Development
c. Cligny	b. Disney	c. Autism
d. Cry too much	c. Dream Catcher	d. Eating Disorder
e. Excessive Sleeping	d. Gangs	e. Non-Verbal
f. Hurt	e. Horror Movies	f. Obesity
g. Jealousy	f. Necromancy	
h. Moodiness	g. Nickelodeon	
i. Nightmares/ Terrors	h. Pennywise (clown)	
j. Orphan/ Adoption	i. Shaman	
k. Schizophrenia	j. Witch Doctor	
l. Ties to objects		
m. Withdrawal		

Health	Miscellaneous	Self-Destruction
a. Cancer b. COVID-19 c. Deafness d. Diabetes e. HIV f. Tooth Decay (witchcraft)	a. Exaggeration b. Lying c. Mental Confusion d. Prejudice	a. Cutting b. Kicking c. Piercings d. Pulling Hair e. Scratching f. Screaming
Victim Mentality	**Acceptance**	**Rebellion**
a. Bad boy/girl b. Bastard c. Chatter Box d. Double-Minded e. Illegitimate f. Insecurity g. Loneliness h. Mind Control i. Rejection Abandonment j. The Past k. Unworthiness	a. Academic Concerns b. Body Image c. Low Self-Esteem **Sexual and Lust** a. Cross Dressing b. Growing up to fast c. Homosexual d. Lilith e. Tendencies f. Homosexuality g. Jezebel h. LGBTQ+ (Pride) i. Molestation j. Promiscuity k. Spirit Spouse l. Transgender	a. Anger b. Conflict c. Curfew/Rules d. Disobedience e. Disrespect f. Stubbornness

Children Personal Hindrance Inventory

Possessiveness	Anger Issues	Abuse
a. Controlling	a. Bitterness	a. Mental
b. Envy	b. Hatred	b. Mistrust
c. Greed	c. Physical with	c. Negativity
d. Jealousy	others	d. Physical
e. Stinginess	d. Premeditated	e. Sexual
f. Unwilling to share	Murder	f. Verbal
	e. Revenge	
	f. Screaming	
	g. Stubbornness	
	h. Temper/Temper Tantrums	
	i. Unforgiveness	
	j. Violence	
Addictions	**Music**	**Bully**
a. Born Drug Addicted	a. 2 Pac	a. Cyber Bullying
b. Cyber Addiction	b. Beyonce	b. Peer Pressure
c. Chemical Addiction	c. Chris Brown	c. School Bullying
d. Behavioral Addiction	d. Harry Styles	
e. Food Addiction	e. Jay Z	
f. Exercise Addiction	f. Michael Jackson	
g. Shopping Addiction	g. Naz X	
h. Thrill-seeking	h. Rihanna	
i. Sexual Addiction	i. Tyga	
j. Screen Violence		

Fears	Behaviors	
a. Anxiety	a. Anxiety	
b. Fear of Death	b. Behavioral Defiance	
c. Fear of Germs	c. Controlling	
d. Fear of man/parents	d. Curiosity	
e. Fear of sickness	e. Deception	
f. Fear of the Dark	f. Depression	
g. Fear of the Unknown	g. Disregard/ Personal Hatred	
h. Making mistakes	h. Hygiene	
i. Not Being Loved	i. Gangster	
j. Not Being Successful	j. Gothic	
k. Not measuring up	k. Insomnia	
l. Paranoia	l. Lying	
	m. Manipulation	
	n. Poor Self Control	
	o. Psychopath	
	p. Restlessness	
	q. Sloth	
	r. Trust	

NOTES

NOTES

APPENDIX SIX

∿

REFERENCE AND RESOURCES

1. **Website:** www.DeliveranceWithPastorHenry.com

2. **Book:** Breaking Chains of Darkness—Dr. James Fent

3. **Workbook:** "Breaking Chains of Darkness Workbook" link is provided on Spiritual Freedom Network website as a free download.

4. **Deliverance with Pastor Henry:** Facebook, You Tube, Rumble.

5. **WUCC 99.9 FM radio stream:** www.999WUCC.com

6. **Radio Stream:** www.999fm.live

7. **Daily Devotional:** "Daily Declarations for Spiritual Warfare"—John Eckhardt

8. **"Deliverance and Spiritual Warfare Manual"**: John Eckhardt

9. **Article by Pastor Conrad Mbewe**: "Why I Can't Believe In Spirit Husbands And Spirit Wives?

Link to Article:
https://africa.thegospelcoalition.org/article/why-i-cant-believe-in-spirit-husbands-and-spirit-wives/

NOTES

NOTES

SIMPLIFIED DELIVERANCE OUTLINE TO FOLLOW

Step 1. Interview the Candidate

Step 2. Adult Personal Hindrance Inventory—Document 001 Front/Back

Step 3. Deliverance Interview Life Data Sheet—Document-002

Step 4. Preparing For Deliverance Session—Deliverance Guidelines Document-003

Step 5. Setup the room for deliverance
Candidate sits in chair against a wall.

Step 6. Chapter 2   Unforgiveness
family, school, employment, church

Step 7. Chapter 3   Bitterness
arthritis, joint pain, body pain, swelling in joints, cancer, strife, division

Step 8.   Chapter 4   Stubbornness
word curses, generational

Step 9.   Chapter 5   Mind Control
inherited, migraine headaches, the Past

Step 10.   Chapter 6   Tentacles of Mind Control
sever the tentacles, anoint with oil, use Sword of the Spirit

Step 11.   Chapter 7   Leviathan (king of pride)

Step 12.   Chapter 8   Leviathan's Shield Demons—protection
on Leviathan's back, stronghold

Step 13.   Chapter 9   Spirit Spouse—Incubus, Succubus, mar
riage, ring, Lilith

Step 14.   Chapter 10   Spirit Pan—sexual sins, masturbation

Step 15.   Chapter 11   Pharaoh—task masters, bricks, blood,
destiny

Step 16.   Chapter 12   Lukewarmness—no need for deliverance

Step 17.   Chapter 13   Pandemic Deliverance—lingering,
breathe, lungs, demons, death

Step 18.   Chapter 14   SRA

Step 19.   Chapter 15   Signs of demon deliverance

NOTES

NOTES

~

HOW TO MAINTAIN YOUR DELIVERANCE. WHAT SHOULD I DO TO KEEP MY DELIVERANCE?

1. To maintain deliverance, you will have to take responsibility for your home, life, and relationship with God.

2. Deliverance is the first battle. The second battle is remaining free. This is a lifelong battle, which is extremely rewarding and effective, but takes time and effort to adjust to and develop as a discipline. Remember, this requires a whole new way of thinking, and a parting from the old ways [activities, behaviors, and attitudes] that opened the door to demons.

3. Deliverance by itself is not a "quick fix" permanent solution. It is relatively quick, but the permanent solution depends on you, and the choices you make post-deliverance. Scripture tells us we are not to love the things of this world, but the things of heaven. This requires a change in thinking

and behavior. Just remember, there is a God, and a Satan. Activities, thoughts, possessions, and attitudes will either be of God, or of Satan.

4. After deliverance, the power the demons once had is broken, but the devil will present new opportunities to sin to see if he can "win" you back, especially in the area(s) you have sinned or struggled previously.

5. Temptations frequently occur right after a successful deliverance. Attacks will come from the outside—not the inside. This makes it easier to resist, but know, too, that the enemy will want you to think nothing changed.

6. Business as usual, it is not. He is fighting an uphill battle, but you must keep the door shut to old ways.

7. They will continue attacking until they realize you are solid in your new life and focused on God's ways. Satan's attacks will happen throughout life, but the hardest, most frequent ones will be immediately following deliverance.

8. "No temptation [trial or attack] has overcome you except such is common to (all) man; but God is faithful, who will not allow you to be tempted beyond what you are able, but with the temptation will also make a way of escape, that you will be able to bear it (I Corinthians 10:13)."

9. Quickly repent and ask for forgiveness if you sin.

10. **Spiritual House Cleaning:** Clean your house of any item(s) not of God. The saying "we are what we eat" can be applied to other things we take into our hearts and minds [music,

movies, books, etc.]. Look at the areas in your life where the enemy operated most, which is where you will be the most sensitive.

a. Antiques of unknown backgrounds (Where was it? Who used it?)
b. Books
c. Good luck items—rosary, rabbit's foot (prayer/faith makes things happen—not luck)
d. Holistic healing/health
e. Meditation, psychic, etc. (Healing and peace comes from the Lord, not someone's philosophy)
f. Music—rock posters, rock or other music with ungodly words, content or ideas
g. New age
h. Ouija boards, tarot cards, etc.
i. Souvenirs of other countries—contain images of idols or symbols of other—current or ancient—gods or religions.
j. Videos—pornography, violent movies
k. Witchcraft/Occult materials
l. Yoga

11. Ask the Holy Spirit to show you things not pleasing to God.

12. Bless the home out loud. This helps protect you, and your home. It is good to do this daily example, "I bless this home and everything in it, in Jesus' name."

Examine and Change Your Activities

13. **TV:** Consider content on TV today—the programs, commercials, words, images, ideas, activities that are socially acceptable. Give it the God test. Also, does the TV distract

you from praying to God, reading His Word, meditating on His desires for your life? If the answer to either is yes, you need to think about the content TV provides and is it worth it?

14. **Internet:** We all know the Internet can be a great tool for learning, but there is a lot of bad content out there, too. Can you use it in a godly way? If not, is it worth it?

15. Develop a consistent prayer life. Pray every day, not just a minute or two. God gave you life, everything you have, and salvation. Think about that when deciding how much time you must pray each day. You may decide other things are less important.

16. Read and study the Bible. This fills the void created after deliverance.

17. Receiving the baptism in the Holy Spirit and speaking in tongues is needed. This is the empowerment of the first century apostles needed to overcome the temptations and attacks of the enemy.

18. Assemble in the church. Get involved in a church of like-minded people.

19. Areas that were strongholds before must be avoided, such as being easily tempted. E.g., if drugs, alcohol, pornography, etc. were issues before, be sure to steer clear of them as well as people and places that will promote these kinds of activities.

20. Put on the armor of God and live it. Put it on daily one piece at a time.

The Armor of God, Ephesians 6:10-18

21. Finally, my brethren, be strong in the Lord, and in the power of his might.

22. Put on the whole armor of God, that ye may be able to stand against the wiles of the devil.

23. For we wrestle not against flesh and blood, but against principalities, against powers, against the rulers of the darkness of this world, against spiritual wickedness in high places.

24. Wherefore take unto you the whole armor of God, that ye may be able to withstand in the evil day, and having done all, to stand.

25. Stand therefore, having your loins girt about with truth, and having on the breastplate of righteousness;

26. And your feet shod with the preparation of the gospel of peace;

27. Above all, taking the shield of faith, wherewith ye shall be able to quench all the fiery darts of the wicked.

28. And take the helmet of salvation, and the sword of the Spirit, which is the word of God.

29. Praying always with all prayer and supplication in the Spirit, and watching thereunto with all perseverance and supplication for all saints.

30. Resist the devil and control your thoughts. Thoughts are like hinges on a door. The more you think about a subject, then one hinge forms. Keep thinking another, then another, then the doorknob appears.

God Has Provided Weapons

31. Plead the Blood of Jesus, use the Word—quote scriptural references out loud, fasting, and prayer [regular and tongues] are all excellent. Praying to the Lord in your head is good, but when praying specific prayers against the enemy and his tactics, the key is to always speak those prayers out loud. Prayer in your head will not affect the enemy attacking on the outside.

32. Spiritual warfare prayers must be spoken out loud daily. The devil will not quit, so the best thing is to start defending first thing in the day.

33. The key battlefield area is the mind, which is how the strongholds are developed. When you have a thought determine if it is Godly thought or not. If not, reject it.

    "For though we walk in the flesh, we do not war after the flesh. For the weapons of our warfare are not carnal, but mighty through God to the pulling down of strong holds; casting down imaginations, and every high thing that exalteth itself against the knowledge of God, and bringing into captivity every thought to the obedience of Christ (II Corinthians 10:3-5)."

34. If you were delivered from anger, for example, rebuke the feelings and thoughts that would lead you to get angry. If you

were delivered from a spirit of infirmity [sickness], rebuke those thoughts/symptoms of sickness.

35. The Bible calls those lying vanities. Rebuke them instead of accepting them. For example, again, say out loud, "In the name of Jesus, I rebuke all feelings of anger, and whatever spirits are trying to make me angry." The enemy will try to make you feel a certain way, but they can only make you feel as much as you let them. Ultimately, the key to lasting victory is to submit yourself to God and resist the devil, and he will flee (James 4:7).

36. Know your authority through the Lord Jesus. The devil was defeated at the cross, and he knows it, but you must come against the enemy each day, exercising your authority. You will win, but to do so you must fight.

37. Know the devil does not play fair. He will try to trick you and put tests in your path. Combat fear, the direct opposite of faith. With full, true faith, there is no fear. Fear is a tactic and tool of the enemy.

38. Self-imposed curses, ungodly beliefs, or curses spoken about others. Idle words are dangerous—the "power of life and death is in the tongue." E.g. "I am always… (sick, for example)," "David never does anything right." If you find yourself saying things like this about yourself or others, or believing it about yourself say, "I rebuke that in the name of Jesus." God did not make us to be sick, confused, forgetful, angry, prideful, etc. Rebuke those thoughts, feelings, and symptoms.

39. Upon waking, say, "I cover myself and my family in the blood of Jesus for our protection, and I forbid the transfer of all evil, wicked, and demonic spirits in the name of Jesus. In the name of Jesus, I put on the full armor of God—the breastplate of righteousness, the sandals of peace, the shield of faith, the helmet of salvation, and I take up the sword of the Spirit."

40. Before entering a store, workplace, etc., "I cover myself and my family with the blood of Jesus for our protection, and I forbid the transfer of all evil, wicked demonic spirits in the name of Jesus.

41. "I bind the strongman in everyone on this property and in this building in the name of Jesus." You will be amazed how effective this is and how it will change your experience with other people.

42. Before speaking with someone on the phone, in person, etc., "I bind the strongman in _____ in the name of Jesus."

NOTES

NOTES

APPENDIX NINE

PRAYERS

These are not mandatory prayers but can be very helpful if the candidate prays them prior to or during the deliverance. The candidate can either read them, pray them in their own words or the deliverance minister can read and have them repeat it. There is no right or wrong way if they are prayed with a sincere heart.

Repentance and Recommitment to Christ

Father, I believe that Jesus is Your Son. He is the Savior come in the flesh to destroy the works of the devil. He died on the cross for my sins and He rose from the dead. I now confess all my sins, known and unknown and repent of each one. I ask You to forgive me and cleanse me by the blood of Your Son Jesus. I do believe His blood cleanses me of all sin. Thank you for redeeming me, cleansing me, and sanctifying me in Jesus' name. Amen!

Commitment to Christ

Heavenly Father, I am Your child, redeemed by the precious blood of Jesus. You have given me life, and I now give my life to you. My heart's desire is to glorify Your Name. I am an ambassador for

Christ and a minister of reconciliation. In Your strength I will love, obey and serve You all the days of my life. Amen!

Forgiveness Prayer

Lord, others have trespassed against me, but in obedience to Your command I now forgive each person who has ever hurt me in any way.

As an act of my will, I now forgive (name living and dead). Lord, I bless each of these individuals; I love them with Your love, and I ask You to forgive them also.

Since You have forgiven me, I also forgive and accept myself in the name of Jesus Christ. The curse of unforgiveness has no more power in my life.

Occult Confession Prayer

Father, I confess as sin and seek Your forgiveness for every occult involvement. I confess having sought from Satan the power that should have only come from You, God. I renounce every occult activity; I renounce Satan and all his works. Father, I loosen myself from Satan, and take back all the ground I have ever yielded to him in Jesus' name.

Loosing From Witchcraft And Related Powers

Father, I now repent of and rebuke, break and loose myself, and my family, from all evil curses operating through charms, vexes, hexes, spells, omens, jinxes, any implements, or tools.

I break all words and actions used against me through psychic powers, predictions, mind control, witchcraft or sorcery that have been put upon me and my family members through any person, or from any cult or occult source.

I command all such demonic powers to leave when told and to go to the pit when addressed in Jesus' name. I am the head and not the tail. I am above and not beneath.

Loosing From Dominion Prayer

Father, I renounce, break, and loose myself from all demonic subjection to or from my mother, my father, my grandparents, and any other human being, living or dead, who has controlled me in any way in Jesus' name. I thank You, Lord, for setting me free.

Breaking Curses Confession

Father, I confess and repent of all the sins of my forefathers, and by the redemptive blood of Jesus.

I now break the power of every word curse passed down to me through my ancestral line. I confess and repent of each sin that I have committed, known or unknown and I accept Christ's forgiveness.

He has redeemed me from the curse of the law, I choose the blessing and I reject the curse. Father, I ask You to lift and break the power of every curse spoken against me.

I ask You to cancel the force of every prediction spoken about me, whether intentionally or carelessly, that was not according to Your promised blessings.

Father, I ask You to bless those who have cursed me and to lift and break the power of every curse - stopping it from going any further down my bloodline. I command every spirit to leave and to go to the pit in Jesus' name.

Breaking Soul Ties

I renounce, break, and loose myself from the kingdom of darkness through ungodly soul ties. Father, I ask You to lift and break all ungodly, demonic soul ties through sinful sexual encounters or other ungodly behavior in which two or more participated.

(Note: Be as specific as possible when breaking soul ties name each person or sexual partner and verbally renounce the tie with each one.)

I accept God's forgiveness for each sin in which I participated. Father, I break all soul ties with: Animals - formed through inordinate affection for animals: Family members - where there is control and possessiveness; Corrupt and depraved companions who have influenced me in perverse ways.

I now break soul ties with the dead and from prolonged mourning over deceased loved ones.

I now break Church related soul ties where I have been a part of church cliques, idolized a pastor or church leader above Christ, or been controlled by anyone in leadership in Jesus' name.

Prayer to Break the Curse of Illegitimacy

Father, I come to You with a repentant heart, as I confess as sin my and/or my ancestor's involvement in illegitimate children. I go back as far as necessary to sever and break this curse over my bloodline in Jesus' name.

I repent for my and/or their behavior for bringing this curse of illegitimacy into the bloodline. I acknowledge that Your Son's blood redeems us from all curses.

I nail the sins, transgressions and iniquities of myself and my ancestors to the cross in Jesus' name. I ask You, Father, to lift and break this curse from me, my spouse, my children, and all future generations.

I ask you to restore the blessings in my life that I can come freely into the congregation and have sweet fellowship with You Father, Your Son, Jesus, the Holy Spirit, and my brothers and sisters in Christ. I thank You for Your faithfulness. In Jesus' name I pray, Amen.

Help me in overcoming the stigma of living under this curse and I ask You to lift and to break any unhealthy habit patterns I inherited or developed. I seal this prayer by the blood of the Lamb, in Jesus' name.

NOTES

NOTES

AUTHOR BIO

Pastor Henry B. Shaffer, Sr., has pastored the University Parkway Church of God in Aiken, South Carolina, for the past twenty-three years. He is married to his wife and best friend of forty-eight years, Fran Wylds Shaffer. He has three children, numerous grandchildren, and a great-grandchild. He began his career at an early age in electrical construction, moving into plant maintenance for major pharmaceutical companies. His supporting roles in electrical, instrumentation, and engineering projects were valuable assets to the success of many projects. He was called into full-time ministry in 2000. In 2003, he led University Parkway Church in a significant building project to establish a new facility in 2005. In 2007, he founded a Christian radio station, WUCC 99.9 fm. By completing the FCC filing and launching the mission in 2014, Shaffer put God's Word on the radio twenty-four hours a day, seven days a week. In 2015, deliverance exploded at University Parkway Church. People have descended upon the church for the last eight years to receive deliverance. They come from all walks of life and across America and the world. In 2016, the ministry Spiritual Freedom Network (SFN) was developed. Pastor Henry is part of the board of directors for SFN Ministry. In 2023, he appeared in the movie, *"Come Out In Jesus Name"* by Locke Media. He is a sought-after speaker and seminar instructor to teach the body of Christ about the ministry of deliverance.

The Fiery Sword Global Ministries
The Fiery Sword Publications
Lexington, SC 29073

www.thefierysword.com
thefierysword@windstream.net

Made in the USA
Columbia, SC
09 November 2024

45683265R00124